W9-CWQ-726

MAKE YOUR OWN
WILL

A GUIDE TO MAKING A MICHIGAN STATUTORY WILL WITHOUT A LAWYER

BY MICHAEL MARAN

Grand River Press
P.O. Box 1342
E. Lansing, MI 48826

Make Your Own Will: A Guide to Making a Michigan
Statutory Will without a Lawyer
by Michael Maran

Published by:
Grand River Press
P.O. Box 1342
E. Lansing, MI 48826

Copyright © 1990 by Michael Maran

All rights reserved. No part of this book may be reproduced or trans-
mitted in any form or by any means without the written permission of
the publisher.

Printing history:
First edition: April, 1990
ISBN 0-936343-04-4

Notice of liability: The information in this book is provided on an "as is"
basis, without warranty. Neither the author nor the publisher shall have
any liability to any person or entity with regard to any liability, loss or
damage caused or alleged to be caused directly or indirectly by the information contained in this book.

Warning: This book contains information that may become obsolete as
laws change.

ORDER FORM

Grand River Press
P.O. Box 1342
E. Lansing, MI 48826

- **Make Your Own Will: A Guide to Making a Michigan Statutory Will without a Lawyer**   **$9.95**

ALSO AVAILABLE:

- **The Michigan Divorce Book: A Guide to Doing an Uncontested Divorce without an Attorney (without minor children)**   **$18.95**

- **The Michigan Divorce Book: A Guide to Doing an Uncontested Divorce without an Attorney (with minor children)**   **$24.95**

- -

Title	Price	Quantity	Total
		Subtotal	
		Sales Tax	
		Postage	
		Total	

ORDERING INFORMATION

- Michigan residents add 4% sales tax.
- Include postage with your order as follows: $2 for the first book ordered and .50 for each additional book.
- Make all checks or money orders payable to Grand River Press.
- Payment by money order will expedite your order.

Name _____

Address _____

City _____ State _____ Zip _____

Acknowledgments:

Artwork:
Altese Graphic Design
3620 S. DeWitt Rd.
Lansing, MI 48906
(517) 321-6788

High Resolution Output:
The Copyfitters, Ltd.
721 N. Capitol
Suite 2
Lansing, MI 48906
(517) 482-7000

TABLE OF CONTENTS

 **Preface**

Years ago, when English lawyers gathered for drinks and good cheer, they had a favorite toast: "To the lawyer's best friend—the man who makes his own will."

These days, a homemade will doesn't have to spell future legal trouble. With the help of simple fill-in-the-blanks form wills like the Michigan statutory will, making your own will can be as safe as having a lawyer prepare one for you. In fact, making a statutory will may be even safer, because a statutory will is a legally authorized and approved form.

Still, you shouldn't flip to the back of this book and try to dash off a statutory will. Take the time to review Chapter 1 to get some background information about wills. Whether you find the dose of will history interesting, this chapter explains what a will can and cannot do.

In Chapter 2, Part I examines some of the limitations of a Michigan statutory will. Part II provides general information and advice about willmaking. Part III guides you through making a statutory will section-by-section. After you make a statutory will, you must "execute" the will (by signing/acknowledging it before witnesses). Part IV tells how you to execute the statutory will that you have made. Finally, Part V has some suggestions about storing your will and revising it in the future.

1 | Introduction to Wills

Making a will is by no means the only way to plan your estate. Gifts, trusts, shared ownership of property and life insurance are other estate planning tools that can do many of the things wills do—and sometimes more. But of all these estate planning devices, wills, through the years, have proved to be the most durable and adaptable.

People are used to thinking of a will as a fussy document that a lawyer prepares for signing before witnesses during a quaint will-signing ceremony. But, the fact is, you really don't need a lawyer to make a will (this book is proof of that), it doesn't necessarily have to be witnessed (at least this is true of a special "holographic" (handwritten) will), and a will doesn't always have to be written in a document (some states, but not Michigan, permit oral wills).

As a matter of fact, wills have come in all shapes and sizes. Wills have been scratched on cocktail napkins, backs of envelopes and other odd scraps of paper. One man passed an estate of $6 million by a will scrawled on a hospital chart. Another hospitalized willmaker chose an even more unlikely place for his will: a nurse's underwear. It seems that the willmaker suddenly decided to make his will and no paper was available. One of the two nurses in attendance offered the white slip under her dress. The willmaker disposed of his estate there, and both nurses signed the garment as witnesses. For their trouble, the nurses were each given a $10,000 gift in the will. The will, dubbed the "petticoat will," was eventually probated after the willmaker's death (although the $10,000 gifts to the nurses were stricken from it because will gifts to witnesses are disfavored). If this weren't odd enough, there have been reports of wills written on the wall of a prison cell, the bark of trees and even a will tattoo!

Wills have been long, and there have been short wills. Newspaper magnate William Randolph Hearst, who was a bit of a windbag during his lifetime, left a will believed to be the longest ever probated in the United States. Hearst's will fills many volumes and takes up several rooms of storage. At the other extreme was the will of a drowned English sailor, which said simply: "All to mother." The sailor's will was carefully etched on his dog tag, and was readable only with the aid of a microscope.

Besides their great flexibility and adaptability, wills are nearly universal. Almost every country allows its citizens to make wills and inherit property. This is true even in many communist countries where the state, at least in theory, owns all property. For example, in the Soviet Union, the Communist Party at first tried to abolish wills and the inheritance of property. After bitter protests, they were eventually restored. Today, the right to inherit personal property is guaranteed by Art. 13 in Chapter 2 of the 1977 Soviet Constitution. (Interestingly, the U.S. Constitution has no such guarantee, so states would probably have the right to restrict or even abolish the ability to will and inherit property if they wished.)

Ancient Wills

Wills have also been around for ages. Scholars speculate that wills and related inheritance laws were devised by primitive people to prevent squabbling over deceased persons' property. In the ancient world, many peoples, including the Egyptians, Greeks and Romans, made wills. In Egypt, archaeologists have discovered what may be the oldest known will, dating from 2601 B.C., inscribed on the wall of a tomb. The will belonged to Nek'ure, son of Pharaoh Khafre, who built one of the pyramids. To give you a taste of ancient willmaking, here is another Egyptian will—a relatively recent one as Egyptian wills go—from the second millenium B.C.:

Will of Uah

I, Uah, am giving a title to property to my wife Sheftu, the woman of Gesab, who is called Teta, the daughter of Sat Sepdu, of all things given to me by my brother Ankh-ren. She shall give it to any she desires of her children she bears me.

I am giving to her the eastern slaves, four persons, that my brother Ankh-ren gave me. She shall give them to whomsoever she will of her children.

As to my tomb, let me be buried in it with my wife alone.

Moreover, as to the house built for me by my brother, Ankh-ren, my wife shall dwell therein without allowing her to be put forth on the ground by any person.

Done in the presence of these witnesses. Kemen, decorator of columns. Apu, doorkeeper of the Temple. Senb, son of Senb, doorkeeper of the Temple.

In many ways, this will is strikingly modern. Like contemporary wills, Uah's will begins by introducing its maker (Uah) and his spouse (Sheftu, the woman of Gesab). It proceeds to dispose of some miscellaneous personal property (the eastern slaves, etc.) and real property (the house that Ankh-ren built). Then Uah decides to make some burial and other final directions. He winds up by mentioning the three witnesses to the will (Kemen, Apu and Senb).

In spite of Egyptian wills' resemblance to modern wills, willmaking didn't really start in earnest until Roman times. The Romans were skillful and enthusiastic willmakers, and the will laws they devised have endured as long as their magnificent roads and buildings. The Roman will began very humbly. At first, Roman "wills" were little more than disguised sales of property by owners to their heirs. The owner, perhaps a father, would declare publicly that he was selling his property to his successor, such as a son. Eventually the sale element of this transaction disappeared, and a property owner was permitted to transfer, effective at death, property to his designees. This was a true will.

By this time, wills were written on parchment or papyrus instead of being carved on walls of tombs or temple columns. Consequently, the Romans provided for a public place where wills could be stored, yet kept confidential, until death. The Romans also adopted strict rules about the signing and witnessing of wills. As it developed, Roman will law also grappled with knotty problems like the disinheritance of spouses and children—problems that vex us even today—and it devised legal protections for family members from disinheritance. By the time Roman will law had undergone its final refinement, in the 6th century A.D. Code of Justinian, the Roman law of wills had become a very subtle and sophisticated thing. In fact, Roman will law was so far ahead of its time that it continued to influence will laws for hundreds of years until even modern times.

English Wills

Despite its vast influence, Roman will law had less impact on England, where most of our will law comes. In medieval England, "wills" affected only real property (land and buildings) while "testaments" passed personal property (all property except land and buildings). During the Middle Ages, feudal principles governed the transfer of most land, leaving wills with little to do. On the other hand, medieval Englishmen could freely dispose of their personal property in testaments, which were subject to more flexible rules derived from the Roman law of wills.

As a consequence, a medieval English estate plan demanded two separate instruments: 1) a will to pass any transferable real property 2) a testament to dispose of personal property. Eventually these instruments were combined into one document known as a "last will and testament." Later, in England's Wills Act of 1837, the distinction between wills and testaments was erased, and the term "will" was adopted to cover the deathtime transfer of all types of property. Notwithstanding this reform, many lawyers persisted in using the word "testament." Even today, one may still find lawyers who designate a will as a "last will and testament," although the latter word is legally meaningless.

When this country was founded, the early colonists brought the English law of wills with them. However, the colonists did not hesitate to adapt that law to suit their own needs. For example, pragmatic Americans saw no need to require two documents to dispose of property after death. Consequently, early American will laws typically permitted willmakers to dispose of all their property—real and personal alike—in wills. But in spite of these differences, American will law continued to be influenced by English law, even after the two countries parted. The English Wills Act of 1837 proved to be particularly influential. Besides abolishing the distinction between wills and testaments, that statute had imposed a number of strict requirements for the writing, signing and witnessing of wills. When American states began devising wills laws in the 19th century, they often emulated the English Wills Act and adopted those same requirements.

Types of Wills

Unlike most countries, the United States has no national law of wills. In this country, wills are regulated by the states' will laws, and each state has its own peculiar will law. To a degree, these laws have grown closer in recent years as many states have begun to standardize their will laws a bit. Even so, many differences persist. Nowhere are there more differences than in the types of wills states permit:

Written wills. Most states require that wills must be written documents. Yet, states permit a wide variety of written wills:

¶ *Ordinary will.* Ordinary wills include the great number of wills that are prepared specially for willmakers and are signed by them before witnesses. Typically, these ordinary wills are prepared by lawyers, although there is no legal requirement for that. However, it appears that few people have dared to make their own wills because only lawyers seem to know the mysteries of will writing and will "execution" (the procedure for signing and witnessing a will).

¶ *Holographic will.* A holographic will is a will that the willmaker has handwritten. Because it can be authenticated by analysis of the handwriting, a holographic will does not require witnesses.

Written Wills

Holographic wills are a creation of Spanish and French law, and they were brought to several southern and western states in this country by Spanish and French settlers there. Holographic wills were generally not recognized in other states, including Michigan. Recently, many of those states have changed their will laws to permit holographic wills. When Michigan revised its will law in 1979, it adopted a provision that allows one to make holographic wills.

¶ *Statutory will.* According to various estimates, somewhere around two-thirds of Americans don't have wills. Apparently, many people have been discouraged from making wills by the cost and trouble of going to lawyers for ordinary wills. To correct this, a handful of states have enacted statutory will laws. Statutory wills are wills whose form and content are prescribed by statute. Since a statutory will is a standardized form, people can make them themselves without lawyers.

California was the first state to enact a statutory will law in 1983, followed by Maine and Wisconsin in 1984. The statutory will laws in California and Wisconsin actually provide for two types of statutory wills: a basic statutory will and a special statutory will with a trust for young children. Bills to create similar statutory wills were introduced in Michigan in 1984. However, lawyers and trust companies feared that the statutory will with trust would take business away from them. They lobbied against that statutory will, and only the basic statutory will was adopted in 1986. The next year, the statutory will with trust bill was reintroduced but it failed to pass during the 1987-88 legislative session. That bill has not been revived since and it seems doubtful that Michigan will have the statutory will with trust anytime soon, if ever.

¶ *Joint will.* A joint will is a will that several people have made together. Years ago, joint wills were popular, particularly among married couples, because they were cheap (you got two wills for the price of one). Yet joint wills had a serious liability: The making of a joint will often legally bound the joint willmakers to the will. This prevented either joint willmaker from changing the terms of the will later, even after the death of one of them. Because of this problem, few people are advised to make joint wills today. Instead, people who want to make wills together, such as spouses, should make their own separate wills. They may, if they wish, make wills whose provisions are similar, but they should do that in separate and independent wills, not joint wills.

¶ *Living "will."* Living wills are not really wills at all. A living will is merely a declaration about whether one wants one's life artificially sustained when death is imminent. Michigan residents sometimes prepare living wills, although Michigan is one of only 11 states that doesn't have a living will law. Advocates of living wills have tried repeatedly to get a living will law enacted in Michigan, but their efforts have failed. Yet, it seems that the trend is in favor of living wills, and that some sort of living will legislation shall be passed in Michigan in the future.

Unwritten wills. In former times, when most people were illiterate, wills were usually unwritten. As often as not, these wills were whispered to friends or relatives upon a willmaker's deathbed. Since such wills were ripe for misinterpretation and abuse, will laws have gradually restricted the making of unwritten wills.

Unwritten Wills

¶ *Oral will.* Because of this tradition of unwritten willmaking, some states have permitted oral wills under special emergency circumstances. For example, several states allowed persons on their deathbeds or military servicemen during war to make oral wills. Before 1979, Michigan permitted oral wills by military servicemen on active duty or by others when the value of the property transferred was small ($300 or less). But since 1979, Michigan, like most states today, has forbidden any sort of oral will.

¶ *Video will.* There may come a day when wills, instead of being written, are recorded on videotape or by other electronic means. Presently, no state permits the videotaping of wills. A few states, such as Indiana, have laws about the videotaping of will executions, although the wills themselves must still be in writing. Michigan does not have any laws relating to the videotaping of wills or will executions.

Benefits of Wills

Despite their long and noble history, wills are probably less important today than they once were. This is because the nature of property ownership has changed over the years, and the type of property a will passes has been declining. You see, a will can dispose of only a willmaker's "probate" property.* In Michigan, probate property includes the following types of assets:

Probate Property

- property owned in your name alone (solely-owned property)
- your % share of tenancy in common property (a type of shared ownership property)
- proceeds from life insurance on your life when you have named your estate as the beneficiary of them
- retirement plan (pension, IRA, Keogh plan, etc.) death benefits when you have named your estate as the beneficiary of them

On the other hand, a will cannot dispose of your "nonprobate" property. When you die, your nonprobate property passes to others according to its own rules, unaffected by your will. For example, joint tenancy property is a type of nonprobate property. One characteristic of joint tenancy property is its "right of survivorship:" When one joint tenant dies, the property passes to the survivor, outside of the deceased's will, estate and probate. Michigan nonprobate property includes the following types of assets:

- shared ownership property other than tenancy in common property:
  - joint tenancy property
  - tenancy by the entirety property (a type of joint tenancy between spouses)

Nonprobate Property

- proceeds from life insurance on your life payable to beneficiaries other than your estate
- retirement plan (pension, IRA, Keogh plan, etc.) death benefits payable to beneficiaries other than your estate
- property held in a "living" (*inter vivos*) trust

---

* This property makes up a person's "estate."

In recent years, nonprobate property has been increasing at the expense of probate property. Where a husband might have once owned the family home solely, today he more likely than not owns it with his wife in joint tenancy or tenancy by the entirety. Life insurance and retirement plans, almost unheard of a 100 or even 50 years ago, nowadays frequently represent the bulk of peoples' wealth. As a result, wills, which do not affect such nonprobate property, are disposing of a decreasing share of peoples' property these days.

Nevertheless, wills are still important transmitters of property. Whether they intend to or not, deceased persons almost always leave some miscellaneous solely-owned property behind. Property you think is owned jointly may turn out to be owned solely. Thanks to a peculiarity of Michigan law, family household furnishings and goods will often wind up the sole property of the husband, even when they have been purchased with family funds. What's more, nonprobate property may eventually lose its character and become converted into probate property. For example, spouses might own some property as joint tenants. When one spouse dies, the joint tenancy property will automatically pass to the surviving spouse. At that point, the surviving spouse will be the sole owner of the property.* In all these cases, the property owners would benefit from having wills to distribute the property to the ones they want.

Besides disposing of property, wills can accomplish a number of other important estate planning goals. In fact, wills are the only means to carry out some of these tasks, such as appointing "fiduciaries" (personal representatives, guardians and conservators for children). Some of the things wills can do include:

Personalize Estate Distribution

For those who die without wills, state inheritance laws provide how the probate property in their estates** shall be distributed. Each state has its own inheritance law, but all the laws have one thing in common: They distribute estates according to rigid patterns. The Michigan inheritance law is no exception in this regard. Its fixed pattern of estate distribution is depicted on the next page.

This pattern of distribution may be dissatisfactory for many people, particularly married couples. These days, it seems that most spouses want to give all or the bulk of their estates to each other, excluding their children or others (although these people may want their children/others to take their estates when their spouses have failed to survive them). In fact, various studies and surveys have confirmed this. They show that married persons

---

* Of course, the surviving spouse could create a new joint tenancy with someone else; but, at some point, a sole owner of the property will remain, who will need a will to direct it to someone else.

** Inheritance laws, like wills, do not touch nonprobate property.

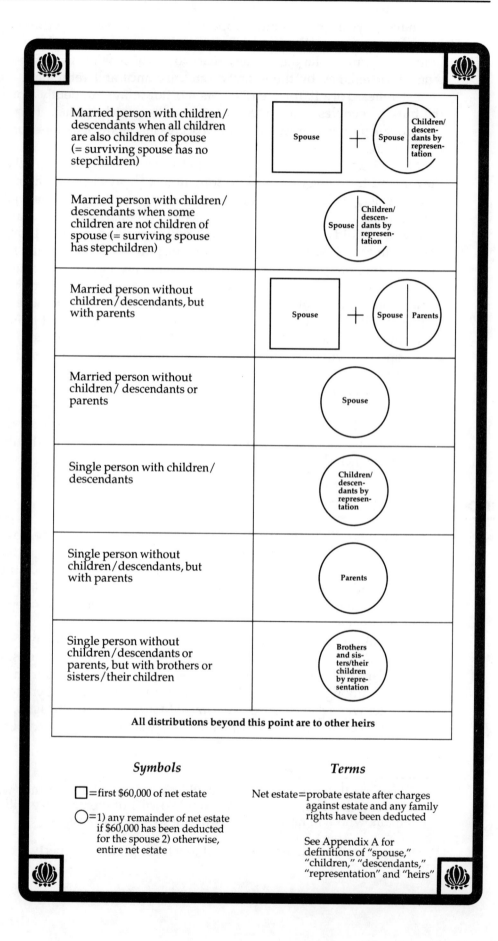

Married person with children/descendants when all children are also children of spouse (= surviving spouse has no stepchildren)	Spouse + Spouse / Children/descendants by representation
Married person with children/descendants when some children are not children of spouse (= surviving spouse has stepchildren)	Spouse / Children/descendants by representation
Married person without children/descendants, but with parents	Spouse + Spouse / Parents
Married person without children/descendants or parents	Spouse
Single person with children/descendants	Children/descendants by representation
Single person without children/descendants, but with parents	Parents
Single person without children/descendants or parents, but with brothers or sisters/their children	Brothers and sisters/their children by representation

All distributions beyond this point are to other heirs

Symbols

☐ = first $60,000 of net estate

◯ = 1) any remainder of net estate if $60,000 has been deducted for the spouse 2) otherwise, entire net estate

Terms

Net estate = probate estate after charges against estate and any family rights have been deducted

See Appendix A for definitions of "spouse," "children," "descendants," "representation" and "heirs" increasingly prefer the "all to spouse, then to children/others" pattern of estate distribution.

Despite this trend, inheritance laws have clung to the notion that at least some of the estate should be kept in the family among blood relatives (of course, a spouse is a relative by marriage, not blood). To an extent, Michigan's inheritance law suffers from that prejudice. It tends to stint the surviving spouse in favor of the children, who may be allotted a sizable share of the estate when it is large (over $60,000). If anything, the situation is even worse for surviving spouses who are also stepparents, because they must split the estate dollar-for-dollar with their stepchildren/children. Likewise, childless spouses may not want their parents, who might be well-fixed financially, to share in their estates along with their surviving spouses.

Others may find the inheritance law distasteful for different reasons. Some parents might want to give their estates to their children in unequal shares; while a few parents may want to disinherit some of their children totally. Persons who are single and have been childless may want their estates to go to their brothers and sisters instead of their parents. Finally, anyone who wishes to benefit nonrelatives, such as friends or charities, will have cause to dislike the inheritance law. Since the law makes distributions to spouses and blood relatives only, it lacks any means for benefiting nonrelatives or charities.

The remedy to all those problems is a will. In a will, you can, subject to a few restrictions, create your own personalized pattern of estate distribution. The pattern you devise in your will might resemble the inheritance law's pattern (most willmakers end up sticking fairly closely to the basic inheritance law scheme, but with a few important adjustments, such as increasing their spouses' shares or by making some gifts to friends or charities).

On the other hand, the pattern of estate distribution you choose could be dramatically different from the one in the inheritance law. Sometimes willmakers even choose odd patterns. One wealthy California farmer gave his farm, worth $250,000, to a waitress in a diner who had been especially kind to him when she had served him a hamburger and cup of coffee 27 years earlier (when the flabbergasted waitress was found and given the farm, she candidly admitted that she remembered nothing of the willmaker, the hamburger or the coffee). Another wealthy man gave his entire estate to a chorus girl, whom he had never met, because he liked her turned-up nose. As odd as these gifts are, they are usually enforceable because courts take pains to carry out the estate distributions willmakers have chosen. As an exasperated English judge muttered after enforcing one eccentric gift, everyone "in disposing of his property, is at liberty to adopt his own nonsense."

It must be pointed out that wills are not the exclusive way to transfer property selectively in that fashion. Gift-giving, the creation of living trusts and shared ownership property are also ways to pass property along to those one chooses. But, unlike wills, they all result in the property owner's losing some control of the property during his/her lifetime. A will, because it becomes operative only at death, gives the willmaker full lifetime use and enjoyment of the property transferred in the will. If s/he likes, a willmaker can even dispose of (consume, sell, give away, etc.) property that has been promised for someone else in the will. What's more, a will is always revocable during the willmaker's lifetime. Consequently, a willmaker can modify or revoke any provision in his/her will, or revoke the will entirely. Because of these characteristics, wills are arguably the most flexible way to transfer property after death.

Make Specific Gifts

You may have noticed that the inheritance law distributes estates quite indiscriminately by value or in shares. As a result, the inheritance law has no means for directing specific items of estate property to particular recipients. Wills can do that. In a will, you can earmark specific items for transfer, effective only upon your death, to designated takers. Willmakers who choose to make these "specific gifts" usually give sums of money or other items of personal property, such as heirlooms, that have special monetary or sentimental value. But this isn't always so, and some willmakers have made very unusual specific gifts in their wills. Perhaps the strangest of all was a gift made by the late John Reed: his head. Mr. Reed, an employee of Philadelphia's Walnut Street Theater for over 44 years, stipulated in his will that his head should be separated from his body and "duly macerated and prepared" into a skull. The skull was given to the theater for use during performances of *Hamlet* as the skull of Yorick. By this gift, Reed guaranteed that he would remain a part of his beloved theater even after his death.

Create Trusts

Benefits of Trusts

Trusts are triangular arrangements in which the trust creator (settlor) gives property to a person or institution (trustee) to hold for the benefit of others (beneficiaries). In most cases, settlors create trusts to furnish support for the trust beneficiaries. In other cases, the creation of a trust can provide important tax and other benefits for the settlor. But some trusts defy any sort of neat classification. Trusts have been set up for high-minded reasons (the Nobel prizes are paid from a trust created by dynamite inventor Alfred Nobel as atonement for the death and destruction his invention had wreaked) and frivolous ones (playwright George Bernard Shaw endowed his considerable fortune on a trust devoted to finding a new phonetic 44-letter English alphabet).

Trusts can be created during a settlor's lifetime (a "living" or *inter vivos* trust), or a trust can commence afterward if the settlor has created a trust within his/her will (a "testamentary" trust). Willmakers who set up testamentary trusts usually do so to support dependents, such as spouses, children or others, after their deaths. Yet, some willmakers use special testamentary trusts as a means to save the two so-called "death taxes" that can be due at death: 1) state inheritance tax 2) federal estate tax. By using special testamentary trusts, wealthy willmakers can shield estates of $600,001 to $1.2 million from the federal estate tax (estates of $600,000 or less are not generally subject to federal estate taxation; see "Absence of Trusts" in Part I of Chapter 2 for more about wills, trusts and death taxation).

Appoint Fiduciaries

When people die, they may require several types of legal representatives to act for them posthumously. These representatives perform such vital tasks as probating one's estate and taking care of any orphaned children. Because these tasks are so important, those chosen to perform them must be completely trustworthy. This is why these representatives are referred to collectively as "fiduciaries," meaning ones in whom the deceased has placed confidence and trust. These fiduciaries include:

Personal representative. A personal representative (known as an "executor" under former Michigan law) is the fiduciary responsible for probating the estate of a deceased person. To probate an estate, a personal representative must establish ("probate") any will the deceased left behind. S/he must collect all the deceased's probate property, pay any charges against the estate, and distribute the remainder to those entitled to it by the deceased's will or the inheritance law (if the deceased died without a will). After the probate is completed, the personal representative's duties end.

Guardian. Parents are the natural guardians of their minor (under age 18) children. When one parent dies, the survivor usually continues as natural guardian. But when both parents are deceased, another guardian must be appointed to take care of the orphaned children. After the appointment, these children would become the "wards" of the appointed guardian.

Types of Fiduciaries

Like parents with their children, guardians have custody and control of their wards. They must provide a home for them and supervise their medical care, education, religious and social activity. In fact, guardians do all that parents do with one very important exception: They have no legal duty to use their own funds to pay for their wards' support. Instead, a guardian supports the ward with: 1) public benefits 2) money from the ward's own estate. Social security is usually the primary public benefit that wards receive. The ward's estate will include any property the ward has gotten from his/her parents through their wills/inheritance law or by nonprobate transfers (such as life insurance proceeds). If the ward's estate is relatively modest, the guardian can manage it for the ward, although the property in the estate remains the ward's own.

Ordinarily, guardianships expire when wards become adults at the age of 18 (they can end sooner when wards become legally "emancipated" by marriage or several other means). However, the following adults may also require guardians:

Legally incapacitated person. An adult who can't take care of himself/herself because of a mental, physical or personal problem.

Developmentally disabled adult. An adult who has a permanent physical or mental impairment (such as mental retardation).

When spouses or parents of legally incapacitated persons are serving as their guardians, they can select guardians to succeed themselves after their deaths. Likewise, parents of developmentally disabled adults have the same right if they are serving as guardians for them.*

Conservator. A guardian's job is to take care of the material needs of his/her ward. As mentioned above, this might involve managing modest amounts of the ward's property. But if the ward's estate is large or difficult to manage, it might require a separate manager: a conservator. A conservator manages a ward's estate like a trustee. When the guardian needs money for the ward's support, the conservator pays money from the ward's estate to the guardian for that purpose. Later, after the ward becomes an adult, the conservator distributes any remainder of the estate to the ward.

When you die without a will, the probate court will make any necessary fiduciary appointments on your behalf after a court hearing. As with any legal procedure, court hearings on these fiduciary appointments can be expensive and time-consuming. There is also the risk that the court will appoint someone who might have been unacceptable to you. For instance, the probate court might appoint as guardian of your children someone whose child-rearing methods and values are unlike your own.

When you make a will, you have the right to appoint fiduciaries in your will. Willmakers invariably appoint personal representatives in their wills. If they have minor children, they will also want to make guardian and conservator appointments. And, under the circumstances described above, some spouses or parents may be able to make guardian appointments for their legally incapacitated or developmentally disabled relatives. By making these appointments, willmakers have more control over their fiduciaries than if they had died without making wills and fiduciary appointments.

But the fact is, will appointments of fiduciaries are not absolutely binding upon probate courts, and they generally reserve the right to appoint others. Guardian appointments carry the most clout, but probate courts can veto these in some cases. Likewise, a probate court must accept the will appointment of a personal representative unless the appointee is unsuitable for reasons that weren't apparent when the will was made. Probate courts have the most discretion in the appointment of conservators.

Nevertheless, in practice, probate courts almost always ratify will appointments of fiduciaries. Typically, those whom deceased willmakers have appointed as personal representatives and guardians can begin to serve almost immediately, without court hearings, simply by filing a few papers with the probate court. Conservators must still obtain formal court

Appointing Fiduciaries in a Will

---

* In either case, the parent/spouse must already be acting as a court-appointed guardian before s/he can name a successor. Without court appointments, parents/spouses do not have the right to select guardians for their legally incapacitated or developmentally disabled relatives.

approval during court hearings, but usually this goes smoothly when the conservator candidates have been appointed in wills.

Give Final Directions

When you make a will, you also have the opportunity to give some final directions. Like fiduciary appointments, these directions are usually not legally binding. Even so, any directions that you make in your will carry some legal and moral weight with the probate court and/or your survivors.

Some willmakers use their wills to make funeral or burial instructions. While this is permissible, wills are not particularly good places to make such instructions. The trouble is, a will is often not read until after a willmaker's funeral and burial. If the will happened to contain funeral or burial instructions, they may go unheeded. For similar reasons, it isn't wise to make "anatomical gifts" (organ donations or gifts of bodies for medical study or research) in your will, although it is legally possible to do so. Instead of making such directions in your will, it's better to make them in separate documents outside the will: 1) so-called "final instructions" for funeral/burial instructions 2) organ donor cards for anatomical gifts.

Mindful of these limitations, willmakers who leave directions in their wills usually choose to give directions about more practical things. They may direct whether their fiduciaries must post bonds to guarantee the careful performance of their duties. Some choose to make directions about the type of probate they want (there are several in Michigan). On the other hand, some willmakers decide to give far more dramatic directions. Peter the Great, Czar of Russia, used his will to explain to his successors why Russia was destined to rule Europe. If this weren't enough, Peter helpfully included step-by-step instructions for achieving that domination!

A wag once observed that "the man who dies without a will leaves lawyers for his heirs." This remark probably exaggerates the benefits of wills (and the risks of not having one), but it does emphasize the basic usefulness of wills. In fact, one can probably say, without exaggeration, that wills can perform more estate planning tasks than any other single estate planning device.

Yet estate planning should not begin and end with the making of a will. As mentioned before, wills have no effect on nonprobate property, so one must plan for the disposition of that important form of property. If you want to make funeral/burial instructions or anatomical gifts, you should prepare the appropriate documents for those things. But whatever else you do to plan you estate, your will shall certainly be the foundation of your estate plan.

Memorial Day, 1989

The Frisbie Family

George and Margo Frisbie are a married couple. George, 48, is a policeman and Margo, 45, manages a convenience store. They have three children: Thelma, 20, Dewey, 15, and Woodrow, 12. Thelma wed recently. She does not have any children, so George and Margo have no grandchildren. The Frisbies are a close-knit family who live in Lake City, Michigan, near Thelma and her husband.

Eugene's Visit, 1988

The Millsap Family

Edith Millsap, 54, is a widow, whose husband died five years ago. Since his death, Edith has gone back to work as a beautician. She has four children: Grover, 34, Eugene, 30, Shirley, 28, and Wanda, 16. Grover has four children; three with his wife Doreen and a son Garth from his first marriage. Eugene has two children. Shirley also has a child, Rhonda, but she was recently divorcd from her husband Gus. All the family live in Michigan except Eugene and family who live in California.

2

Part I

The Michigan Statutory Will

This book is based on only one type of will: the Michigan statutory will. As explained in Chapter 1, a statutory will is a will whose form and content have been prescribed by statutory law. Since it's a standard form, a statutory will is easy and safe to make—even without a lawyer. However, this simplicity comes at a price: inflexibility. Although a statutory will gives you some choices, it is basically a one-size-fits-all form. Moreover, modification of a statutory will is absolutely prohibited (such modifications could invalidate parts of the will or even the entire will). As a result, statutory willmakers have no choice but to accept their statutory wills' provisions. Needless to say, before you make a statutory will, you must determine if it suits your needs. This section will examine some of the situations in which a statutory will may be unsuitable.

Estate Distribution

Like the inheritance law, a statutory will provides for a fixed pattern of estate distribution. This pattern is not quite as rigid as the inheritance law's pattern (for example, a statutory will gives you two choices about the disposition of your estate if you leave no close family). Nevertheless, a statutory will's pattern of estate distribution is basically fixed and not subject to major change. This pattern is depicted below:

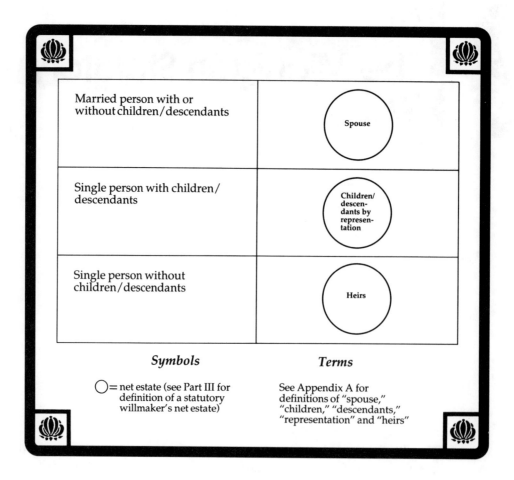

Married person with or without children/descendants	**Spouse**
Single person with children/descendants	**Children/descendants by representation**
Single person without children/descendants	**Heirs**

Symbols

◯ = net estate (see Part III for definition of a statutory willmaker's net estate)

Terms

See Appendix A for definitions of "spouse," "children," "descendants," "representation" and "heirs"

Fortunately, a statutory will's pattern of estate distribution is a popular one that most people want. As mentioned in the first chapter, nowadays married persons seem to prefer to give their entire estates to their spouses, to the exclusion of their children/descendants. Single persons with children/descendants usually want to give their estates to them. And presumably most single persons without children/descendants would want to benefit their heirs (their closest relatives). Yet, despite the popularity of a statutory will's pattern of estate distribution, it might not be right for everyone. It's your responsibility to decide whether that pattern distributes your estate exactly as you want.

Specific Gifts

In other states' versions of the statutory will, one can make a substantial number of specific gifts. For instance, Wisconsin statutory willmakers can make up to five specific gifts of cash or other personal property. And Maine's statutory will permits its users to make a whopping five specific gifts of real property, five specific gifts of personal property and three specific gifts of cash to charities! By comparison, the Michigan statutory will allows you to make a maximum of two specific gifts of cash only.

However, you can compensate for that limitation by making specific gifts outside your statutory will in a "separate list." When you make a separate list, you can make an unlimited number of specific gifts of your "personal and household items" to particular recipients. See Appendix B for more about making a separate list.

Absence of Trusts

As mentioned in Chapter 1, when statutory wills were proposed in Michigan, there were originally two versions: a basic statutory will and a statutory will with trust. The proposed statutory will with trust provided a simple trust for a willmaker's young orphaned children. The trust managed the children's property and provided funds for their "health, support, maintenance and education." The trust continued until the youngest child reached the age of 21, when any remaining trust property was to be turned over to the children. Regrettably, the statutory will with trust was not adopted and is not available in Michigan.

Despite the absence of a trust in the statutory will, it does allow you to appoint a conservator for your minor children. Although a conservatorship is only a partial substitute for a trust, it does some of the same things. Like a trustee, a conservator manages property for a child's (ward's) benefit. After the conservatorship ends (when the ward attains the age of 18), any remaining property is distributed to him/her.

Death Taxes

One thing the statutory wills were never designed to do is save state or federal death taxes. But this might not be a serious deficiency for most statutory willmakers. These days, the federal estate tax has several generous "exemptions" including: 1) an unlimited marital exemption 2) a $600,000 general exemption. Married persons can use the marital exemption to transfer an unlimited amount of property to their spouses without estate taxation. For transfers to nonspouses, the general exemption applies to exempt transfers up to $600,000. Like its federal counterpart, Michigan's inheritance tax also provides an unlimited marital exemption. To be sure, the inheritance tax's general exemptions are not as generous as the federal one. Yet, the inheritance tax rate is quite low (from 2% to 17%), so the tax should not be a big worry for people of modest means.*

What all this means is that most single persons or married couples with total wealth of $600,000 or less do not face significant death taxation, and they probably don't need wills with death tax-saving testamentary trusts. Persons or couples possessing more than $600,000 of wealth may need those

---

*   In recent years, several states have repealed their inheritance taxes. There have been efforts to do the same in Michigan (in fact, a repeal bill is currently pending in the legislature). There's no telling whether Michigan's inheritance tax will be repealed, but there is a chance that it might sometime during the next few years.

trusts, and they should not use statutory wills if they want to avoid unnecessary death taxation.

Appointment of Fiduciaries

A statutory will gives you the opportunity to appoint personal representatives, guardians and conservators. You can also appoint substitutes to serve in those roles when your first choices are unable or unwilling to serve. Despite those provisions, a statutory will possesses several minor limitations when it comes to making fiduciary appointments.

Sometimes willmakers want to make "joint" fiduciary appointments. By making a joint appointment, a willmaker has several appointees join together to fulfill a fiduciary role. For example, one would have joint

appointments by naming co-personal representatives, co-guardians or co-conservators. A statutory will doesn't permit joint appointments because it allows for only one appointee per fiduciary position. Nevertheless, this may not be a serious limitation for most willmakers. There's an old proverb that "three executors make three thieves," meaning that multiple fiduciaries are no guarantee that things will go better than they would with just one. Besides, joint appointments can create practical problems as well.

Example: George and Margo go to a lawyer and have ordinary wills prepared. They name George's brother Chester and his wife Selma as co-guardians of their children. George and Margo die and Chester and Selma become co-guardians of Dewey and Woodrow. Chester wants to transfer the boys to a private school, while Selma wants to leave them in a public school. Their dispute ends up in court, where the probate court decides that the boys should be left in the public school.

Example: Later, Chester and Selma separate and divorce. Each wants to remain guardian of Dewey and Woodrow. Once again, a probate court hearing would have to be held to decide who shall become the sole guardian of the children.

On the other hand, there are some situations in which joint appointments make sense. For instance, a willmaker might appoint a close relative, who has no financial expertise, and a financial expert, such as a friend or financial institution, as his/her joint personal representatives. With this arrangement, the personal attention of the close relative would complement the financial expertise of the other appointee.

In a joint fiduciary appointment, several appointees combine to carry out a fiduciary role. A willmaker can also create a "split" fiduciary appointment by dividing a fiduciary role among several appointees, who perform their tasks separately. For example, one could split a guardian appointment by appointing different guardians for one's children. Split appointments are possible only for guardians and conservators because you cannot split a personal representative's duties. At any rate, a statutory will does not permit any type of split appointment. But like joint appointments, split appointments are usually unnecessary, except in unusual situations.

> *Example*: George and Margo want to name George's brother Chester as guardian for their children, but Dewey has never gotten along with Chester. Dewey does like George's other brother, Wesley. George and Margo decide to make ordinary wills and split their guardian appointments: Chester for Woodrow and Wesley for Dewey.

As mentioned in Chapter 1, spouses or parents of legally incapacitated persons and parents of developmentally disabled adults can appoint successors to succeed themselves as guardians when they are already serving as guardians for these individuals (see "Appoint Fiduciaries" in the first chapter for more about this). However, a statutory will's guardian appointment section is restricted to appointments of guardians for one's *children* (minor or adult) only. Consequently, you cannot use a statutory will to appoint a guardian for your legally incapacitated spouse, as you might be able to do in other types of wills.

Final Directions

Unlike some types of wills, a statutory will gives you scant opportunity to give final directions. A statutory will does allow you to direct whether your fiduciaries must post bonds. Besides that, a statutory will has no room to give other directions, such as funeral/burial instructions or anatomical gifts. Yet, as explained in Chapter 1, it's probably better to make funeral/burial instructions or anatomical gifts outside wills in separate documents anyway (see "Give Final Directions" in Chapter 1 for more on this). As a result, a statutory will's deficiencies with regard to final directions may not be a serious problem.

Conclusion

As you can see, the Michigan statutory will has some shortcomings and limitations. Despite its negatives, a statutory will is still a good simple will that should be suitable for most people. But if you have discovered that a statutory will doesn't suit your needs, don't hesitate to reject it. A will is your chance to do what you want with your estate, so you shouldn't let a will form dictate to you. If you have any misgivings about the statutory will, consider making an ordinary or holographic will instead.

2

Part II

Before You Make Your Statutory Will

A statutory will contains several notices, warnings and instructions about its preparation. Yet this information does not really tell you all you need to know about making your statutory will. This part has information about willmaking in general and making a statutory will in particular. Please review it carefully before you begin making your statutory will.

Who Can Make a Statutory Will?

Mental Capacity

Only people make wills; governments, businesses and other organizations cannot make them. In Michigan, any adult (a person 18 years of age or older) of "sound mind" can make a will. The phrase "sound mind" has a very special meaning in will law. In one sense, it means that a willmaker must have the proper mental capacity to make a will. To have this mental capacity, a willmaker must possess:

- the ability to know the "natural objects of his/her bounty" (the persons whom a willmaker would be expected to benefit, such as close relatives)
- the ability to know the nature and extent of his/her estate
- the ability to understand that s/he is providing for the disposition of his/her estate in the will

- the ability to know the manner in which the the will disposes of his/her estate

When a willmaker is oblivious to any one of those factors, s/he lacks the proper mental capacity to make a will. Moreover, a willmaker, to have a sound mind, must not suffer from an "insane delusion" when s/he makes a will. An insane delusion is a belief in things that have no basis in reality. If such a delusion influenced how a willmaker disposed of property in his/her will, the willmaker's mind might not be sound. Whenever willmakers make wills while they have unsound minds, their wills are completely invalid.

Undue Influence, Duress and Fraud

Besides having a sound mind, a willmaker must make his/her will in the absence of: 1) undue influence 2) duress 3) fraud. A will, by its very nature, is supposed to be the willmaker's voluntary act. If others have influenced the willmaker to the extent that the will is not really his/her free choice, there may have been undue influence. When it occurs, undue influence usually comes from those one holds in special trust or confidence, such as spouses, parents, children or advisers. Duress is like undue influence, but with duress the willmaker is actually forced (usually by physical force or the threat of it) to make the will. A fraudulent will is one based on a misrepresentation (falsification) of a fact which the willmaker has relied on in making his/her will. Wills/will provisions based on undue influence, duress or fraud are invalid.

Residency

In addition to those general willmaking requirements, you should also be a Michigan resident* when you make a Michigan statutory will. As mentioned in Chapter 1, willmaking is regulated by the will laws of the individual states. Consequently, nonresidents of Michigan who try to make a Michigan statutory will might not end up with a valid will. On the other hand, Michigan residents' statutory wills should be recognized in other states—even those without statutory wills—because all states have will reciprocity laws. According to these laws, a will is good anywhere if it was valid when and where it was made. As a result, Michigan statutory willmakers who move to other states will find that their statutory wills are valid there.**

Although you should be a Michigan resident when you make a Michigan statutory will, you don't have to be present in the state when you make your will. For example, you could make your statutory will outside Michigan during a temporary absence, such as a vacation or business trip, from the state. Military servicemen from Michigan should be able to make Michigan statutory wills wherever they are stationed because servicemen ordinarily remain residents of the state they resided in immediately before their enlistment. Finally, persons residing in Michigan who are not U.S. citizens also can make Michigan statutory wills. Their wills should be recognized

---

* Residence is the place where you live either permanently or regularly.

** When you move to another state, you should still review your will. See Part V for more about this.

throughout the United States because of the will reciprocity laws mentioned above. But noncitizens who still have ties to their native countries might want to check with embassies or consulates of their countries to see if their wills shall be recognized there.

Specific Gifts

As mentioned in Part I of this chapter, you can make up to two specific gifts of cash in a statutory will. What's more, you can make additional specific gifts of your "personal and household items" in a separate list. Review the section below before you make either type of specific gift. When you want to make specific gifts in a separate list, see Appendix B for more information and instructions.

Who Can Take a Specific Gift?

You can make specific gifts to any person, including someone who is a minor. If the gift-taker is still a minor at the time for the distribution of the gift, Michigan law says that it shall be distributed to:

- the minor's conservator, if s/he is known to have one
- for "small" gifts (money or other personal property with a value of $5,000 or less annually), the gift will be transferred to: 1) the minor's custodian (a parent or guardian)* 2) the minor personally when the minor is married

Specific Gift-Takers

Specific gifts to adult takers who are mentally or physically incapacitated can be made in a similar way. They would be distributed to the person's guardian or conservator when s/he has one. Finally, you can make specific gifts to persons who don't reside in Michigan or are not U.S. citizens. At one time there were some restrictions about making will gifts to noncitizens, particularly those living in communist countries, but those restrictions have been abolished.

Besides giving to people, you can make specific gifts to a variety of organizations. A statutory will says that you can make specific gifts to "persons or charities." Presumably, "charities" would include do-good organizations like charitable foundations, religious and service organizations. However, you should also be able to make specific gifts to other noncharitable organizations, such as schools, foundations, governments, business and nonprofit organizations, fraternal associations and political parties. Although these organizations might not be able to take your gifts as "charities," they should qualify as "persons" to whom you can benefit with

---

* If the gift is larger, the minor may need a conservator to manage it for him/her.

specific gifts. The sole restriction on giving to organizations is that the organization must have some formal legal identity. You cannot make specific gifts to informal organizations, such as your softball or bowling team, because they are not legally capable of taking your gifts.

One final restriction on making specific gifts is perhaps worth mentioning: You cannot make gifts directly to animals. Such is the affection of people toward animals, especially pets, that willmakers have occasionally violated that rule and made specific gifts to furry beneficiaries. In 1968, Eleanor Ritchey, heiress to the Quaker State Motor Oil fortune, left $4.5 million to her 150 stray dogs. The late Jonathan Jackson was nearly as generous to his pets, this time cats. Mr. Jackson left a sum of money to his cats from which a special "cat-house" was to be built for them. Jackson's will contained detailed instructions for the design of the cat-house, which included a sleeping area, exercise yard, infirmary and a music room where the cats were to be serenaded with accordion music for no less than one hour daily! Actually, if you want to benefit animals in your statutory will, you can make a specific gift to an animal care organization. But to benefit particular animals, such as your pets, you should see a lawyer about creating a special trust for the animals in an ordinary will.

Making Specific Gifts

Whomever you choose to make specific gifts to, you must identify them precisely in your will. Sometimes persons taking specific gifts, particularly relatives, have names that are the same as, or similar to, the names of others. Likewise, charities or other organizations may have like-sounding names. What is worse, the correct legal name of an organization may be quite different from its popular name. Before you make a specific gift, find out the taker's correct name and address. After you have this information, use the taker's full legal name and address in the gift.

If you fail to do that, there may be confusion about who is really entitled to take your specific gift. This can be disastrous when it comes time to distribute the gift. For instance, in one notorious California case, a willmaker left a $5 million gift to the "Society for the Prevention of Cruelty to Animals (local and national)." Because there was no organization that fit that description exactly, some 60 animal care organizations applied for the gift. Their claims had to be sorted out during a lengthy and costly lawsuit.

Initial Selection of Fiduciaries

Before you make your statutory will, you should select the persons or institutions who shall serve as your fiduciaries. The following sections describe some general qualifications for fiduciaries. On the basis of this information, you should be able to narrow the field of fiduciary candidates to several. Yet before you make your final selection, you should review the sections of Part III that deal with the specific qualifications for the various types of fiduciaries.

At the least, you should appoint personal representatives. Willmakers who have minor children shall also want to appoint guardians and conservators for them.* Like all good wills, a statutory will's fiduciary appointment section has provisions for appointing substitute choices for each fiduciary position. These substitutes can take over when your first choice cannot or will not serve. Consequently, you should select two choices for each fiduciary position: a first choice and a substitute.

Fiduciaries: Legal Eligibility

You can appoint any adult person, except someone who is mentally incompetent, to serve as your fiduciary. Ordinarily, you should not appoint minors because they cannot serve as fiduciaries if they are still underage when the time comes for them to assume their duties. Michigan used to bar residents of other states or countries from serving as fiduciaries in many circumstances. But with the mobility of families these days, those rules proved to be much too restrictive. In 1984, they were changed and nonresidents can now serve as fiduciaries in most cases. Likewise, noncitizens (whether residents or nonresidents of Michigan) can also be appointed and serve as fiduciaries.

You can also appoint some financial institutions as personal representatives or conservators. To be eligible for these appointments, a financial institution must have: 1) "trust powers" 2) its principal place of business in Michigan. Only banks and savings and loan associations can get trust powers (although not all such institutions have them). Credit unions and other financial service companies cannot obtain trust powers, so they are ineligible to serve as fiduciaries. Your choice of financial institutions will also be confined to Michigan banks and savings and loans because only they have their principal places of business in Michigan. When you are in doubt about whether a financial institution satisfies those requirements, ask the institution to confirm its eligibility.

Fiduciaries: Practical Qualifications

As you can see, most people and some institutions are legally eligible to serve as fiduciaries. But, for practical reasons, some make better choices than others. The following are a few of the practical qualities that you should look for in a fiduciary:

Honesty. Honesty is by far the most important quality because a fiduciary often handles money or other property. Although a fiduciary acts under the supervision of a probate court, the supervision is not that close. As a consequence, a dishonest fiduciary can do considerable harm before detection and removal. The selection of an honest fiduciary should also allow you

---

*   As mentioned before, in some cases you can also appoint guardians
     for your legally incapacitated or developmentally disabled adult
     children.

to waive (forgo) a bond for the fiduciary, which can save the cost of a bond premium.

Suitability. Fiduciary candidates should be generally suited to the tasks that they will be expected to perform. This doesn't necessarily mean that the candidate must have special expertise, but the candidate should have some aptitude for the job. For instance, someone who has bad business judgment would make an unsuitable personal representative or conservator, just as one who dislikes children would be a poor choice as guardian.

Willingness. A fiduciary's job is strictly voluntary. A fiduciary can decline to serve before appointment or resign afterward. To prevent this, you should always ask all fiduciary candidates whether they would be willing to serve before you appoint them in your will. When you want to appoint financial institutions as fiduciaries, you should always ask them because they might not wish to serve if the estate is too small or hard for them to manage.

Availability. The fiduciaries you select should be from among those whom you expect will be around at your death. Ordinarily, the persons you choose should be around your age, younger or otherwise in good health. Financial institutions wouldn't seem to have this problem, but banks and savings and loan associations have been know to fail. Perhaps you might want to make sure that any institution you appoint is in financial "good health."

Although nonresidents of Michigan are legally eligible to serve as fiduciaries, they may often find it difficult to carry out fiduciary duties long-distance. Consequently, you may want to give preference to candidates who live near you in Michigan.

Besides these qualities, there remains one final consideration for fiduciary appointments: affordability. If an otherwise eligible and qualified fiduciary is going to be too expensive, that candidate should not be chosen. For instance, financial institutions or professionals (lawyers, accountants, financial advisers, etc.) may rate highly on the above factors, but their fiduciary fees may be too costly.

Fiduciary Fees

Years ago, willmakers sometimes gave their personal representatives will gifts to guarantee that they would carry out their wills. Thankfully, you no longer need to "bribe" your fiduciaries that way. Nowadays, fiduciaries are entitled to fees for their services. Willmakers can set fiduciary fees in their wills, although that is seldom done (there is no place to do it in a statutory will). Instead, fiduciaries apply to the probate court periodically for fees. The probate judge must consider the fiduciary's request for fees and grant them in an amount s/he "deems to be just and reasonable." The reasonableness of fiduciary fees depends on several factors, including: 1) the difficulty of the tasks 2) the time spent on them 3) any "fee schedule" the fiduciary uses. Institutional and professional fiduciaries have customarily used fee schedules to figure their fees as a percentage of the estate. If the percentages are high, these fee schedules can result in very stiff fees. However, probate judges provide some check on this because they can reject any fee requests that they believe to be unreasonable.

In some cases, fiduciaries agree to waive the fees to which they are entitled. Close relatives serving as guardians or conservators might waive their fiduciary fees because they know that these fees come out of their wards' estates. A personal representative who is also a taker of the estate, such as a spouse or child, may often waive their fees for a more selfish reason. You see, fiduciary fees are taxable as income to a fiduciary, while any estate distributions to them are not. By waiving their fees, personal representative-estate takers can, in effect, recoup the waived fees by having a larger estate to take (because it hasn't been reduced by fiduciary fees), without income taxation (since estate distributions are income tax-exempt). Needless to say, institutional or professional fiduciaries don't have those incentives for fee waivers, and they probably won't consent to waiving their fees.

Selecting Witnesses for the Execution of Your Will

Besides the initial selection of fiduciaries, you should also think about who will be available to serve as witnesses for your will. These witnesses must observe you as you sign/acknowledge your will (this procedure is known as the "execution" of your will). After your death, during probate, the witnesses may be asked to testify about the execution of your will.* In Michigan, all wills, except holographic wills, must have at least two witnesses. A will without the required minimum two witnesses is invalid. Although only two witnesses are legally required, it's better to use three witnesses when a third witness is available. The extra witness may come in handy if testimony about the will is required and the other two witnesses are unavailable.

Disinterested Witness

Your witnesses must be mentally competent adults. They should also be persons who don't have an interest in your will. The law prefers such "disinterested" witnesses because they, by not having a stake in your will, are inclined to be more objective about the will if they should have to testify about it later during probate. In Michigan, persons who take any sort of distribution from your will or any separate list you make have an interest in your will. These takers would become "interested" witnesses if they were to witness your will. On the other hand, Michigan law does not consider the receipt of fiduciary fees to be an interest in a will because fiduciaries earn their fees by performing services. Consequently, fiduciary appointees can qualify as disinterested witness as long as they don't take any distributions from the will or any separate list.

---

*   Michigan has very liberal rules about probating wills, and the testimony of witnesses is seldom required to probate wills.

Example: George makes a statutory will in which he gives cash gifts to his two brothers. He discovers that Margo and his brothers should not act as witnesses because they, as takers of his estate under the will, would be interested witnesses.

Instead, George takes the will to work and has three of his friends, Archie, Guy and Luther, witness his signing of the will. None of them takes anything from the will or the separate list George has made, although Archie has been appointed as a conservator.

In the above example, George's three friends would be qualified to witness his will because they are all disinterested in it. This is true even of Archie because, as mentioned above, his fiduciary appointment does not provide him with a true interest in the will.

George's Bowling Team, 1987

According to a few earlier will laws, the use of interested witnesses was sometimes fatal to wills. But according to Michigan will law, interested witnesses do not affect the validity of the entire will. If an interested witness is an extra unnecessary witness, the will and the will distribution to the interested witness are valid. For example, if a will had two disinterested witnesses and one interested witness, the will distribution to the interested witness would be permissible because the interested witness is unnecessary (the pair of disinterested witnesses represent the required two witnesses). If an interested witness is one of only two witnesses to a will, just the will distribution to the interested witness is tainted, while the rest of the will remains unaffected. In that case, Michigan law says that the interested witness must take the lesser of: 1) the will distribution 2) whatever the inheritance law gives him/her. Despite the flexibility of these rules, it's always best to use disinterested witnesses only because the use of interested witnesses could upset one's intended pattern of estate distribution.

> *Example*: George makes a statutory will in which he makes a cash gift of $1,000 to his friend Luther. George disregards the rule about having disinterested witnesses and signs the will before Margo and Luther.
>
> Because Margo is an interested and necessary witness, she would be limited to the lesser of: 1) the will distribution to her (George's entire estate) 2) what the inheritance law gives her (the first $60,000 and one-half the remainder of his estate). By the same token, Luther is also an interested and necessary witness, so he gets the lesser of: 1) the will distribution to him (the $1,000 cash gift) 2) what the inheritance law gives him (nothing, because he is not an heir of George). As a result, Margo gets only a fraction of what the will gave her and Luther gets nothing, both contrary to what George wanted in his will.

Aside from the legal qualifications for witnesses, you should, as a practical matter, select witnesses who are likely to be around at your death. Ideally, they should be persons who live near you and are not inclined to move far away. Your witnesses should be around your age, younger or otherwise in good health. As a general rule, your friends usually make the best witnesses because they are often disinterested in your will and are persons with whom you are likely to stay in touch with in the future.

General Instructions about Making a Statutory Will

The next part shows you how to complete a statutory will section-by-section. But before you do that, you should know about some general rules for making a statutory will:

- Use a typewriter or pen with dark permanent ink to make your statutory will. Never use a pencil or a pen with erasable ink.

- Whenever you fill a blank requiring "Your Signature," you must sign your name longhand as you would sign a check. The witnesses must also sign that way in the blanks designated "Signature of Witness."

- Your name in the title of the will and the names of the witnesses in the statement of witnesses section must be printed, not written, by hand or typewriter. Apparently, these names must be printed in those places for the sake of clarity.

- The rest of the blanks can be completed by either printing (by hand or typewriter) or writing. All must be legible, so if your writing is bad you might want to consider printing instead.

- When you identify any person, organization or financial institution in your will, use their full legal names (and addresses, if called for) to avoid confusion about their identities.

- Whenever the name of a person or financial institution appears more than once in your will, the form of the name should be consistent throughout the will. For example, if you use your middle name rather than your middle initial (as you should, see above) in the title of your will, you should use that same form of your name for any signatures in articles 2 and 3 and for your final signature at the end of the will.

- If you don't use a section of your statutory will, just leave it blank. Don't cross out or line out the unused section.

- Don't attempt to customize your statutory will by crossing out words or adding new ones to the form. At best, these changes will be ineffective. At worst, they may result in the invalidity of the modified provision or even the entire will. If the statutory will doesn't suit your needs, don't use it!

2 Part III
Making Your Statutory Will

With the willmaking rules from Part II in mind, you are ready to make your statutory will using one of the statutory will forms from the end of this book (two forms are included for married couples). You should use this part to guide you in completing articles 1-3 of a statutory will. Afterward, you must execute your statutory will. Part IV has information and instructions about will executions.

MICHIGAN STATUTORY WILL

NOTICE

1. Any person age 18 or older and of sound mind may sign a will.
2. There are several kinds of wills. If you choose to complete this form, you will have a Michigan statutory will. If this will does not meet your wishes in any way, you should talk with a lawyer before choosing a Michigan statutory will.
3. Warning! It is strongly recommended that you do not add or cross out any words on this form except for filling in the blanks because all or part of this will may not be valid if you do so.
4. This will has no effect on jointly-held assets, on retirement plan benefits, or on life insurance on your life if you have named a beneficiary who survives you.
5. This will is not designed to reduce inheritance or estate taxes.
6. This will treats adopted children and children born outside of wedlock who would inherit if their parent died without a will the same way as children born or conceived during marriage.
7. You should keep this will in your safe deposit box or other safe place. By paying a small fee, you may file the will in your county's probate court for safekeeping. You should tell your family where the will is kept.
8. You may make and sign a new will at any time. If you marry or divorce after you sign this will, you should make and sign a new will.

INSTRUCTIONS:

1. To have a Michigan statutory will, you must complete the blanks on the will form. You may do this yourself, or direct someone to do it for you. You must either sign the will or direct someone else to sign it in your name and in your presence.
2. Read the entire Michigan statutory will carefully before you begin filling in the blanks. If there is anything you do not understand, you should ask a lawyer to explain it to you.

A statutory will starts with a notice section that tells you that you are making a Michigan statutory will. There are also several notices and instructions about willmaking and what a statutory will can and cannot do. Most of this information has been covered already in earlier parts of this book, but you may want to review it again here. The information in this section about will execution and storage is dealt with later in Parts IV and V of this chapter.

MICHIGAN STATUTORY WILL

of

<u>GEORGE EDWARD FRISBIE</u>
(Print or type your full name)

Title

A statutory will begins in earnest with its title in this section. Like any written work, a will should have a title. This section allows you to entitle your will as the "Michigan Statutory Will of [you]." If you are unsure about how to fill in this or other lines of the will, review "General Instructions about Making a Statutory Will" in Part II.

ARTICLE 1. DECLARATIONS

This is my will and I revoke any prior wills and codicils. I live in <u>OJIBWAY</u> County, Michigan.

My spouse is <u>MARGO ANN FRISBIE</u>
(Insert spouse's name or write "None")

My children now living are:

<u>THELMA MARIE STRANGE</u>
(Insert names or write "None")

<u>DEWEY DONALD FRISBIE</u>

<u>WOODROW ANDREW FRISBIE</u>

Article 1 of the statutory will asks you to make several factual declarations about your personal situation and family. In the old days, introductory will paragraphs such as this were much more colorful, and willmakers frequently began their wills with dramatic prayers or confessions. Like many wills of that time, Shakespeare's will began: "In the name of God Amen...I commend my soul into the hands of God my Creator...and my body to the earth whereof it is made." Later, it became customary for willmakers to introduce their wills by declaring that they were "of sound mind and disposing memory."

By contrast, a statutory will's introductory paragraph is much more business-like. Article 1 has you simply state that this will is your will and that you revoke any prior wills and codicils (will supplements) that you have made. You must also declare the Michigan county of your residence. As mentioned in "Who Can Make a Statutory Will?" in Part II, you should be a

Michigan resident when you make a Michigan statutory will. This declaration helps establish your residency in Michigan for that purpose.

Article 1

Article 1 also has you identify your spouse and children, if any. Your spouse is the person to whom you are *legally* married at the time you sign your will (see Appendix A for more on the legal definition of "spouse"). As for children, a statutory will adopts the standard legal definition of children. Besides children born during a marriage, that definition includes adopted and many illegitimate children, but excludes stepchildren (see Appendix A for more about the legal definition of "children"). When you identify these children in article 1, list only the ones who are living. Your deceased children should be omitted because they will take nothing from your statutory will (although, as explained below, their children/descendants might). Single and/or childless willmakers should put "None" in the appropriate lines in article 1.

If those provisions seem complicated, pity poor Brigham Young, the Mormon leader. At his death, he had 18 living wives, 3 deceased wives and 48 children by them. He also had an unknown number of other secret "wives" according to the Mormon rite. Aware of his domestic entanglements, Young wisely devoted a large portion of his will to defining exactly what he meant when he used the terms "spouse" or "children" in his will!

2.1 CASH GIFTS TO PERSONS OR CHARITIES. (Optional)

I can leave no more than two (2) cash gifts. I make the following cash gifts to the persons or charities in the amounts stated here. Any inheritance tax due shall be paid from the balance of my estate and not from these gifts.

Full name and address of person or charity to receive cash gift. (Name only one (1) person or charity here)

(Please print) __POLICEMEN'S BENEVOLENT FUND__
(Insert name)

of __121 S. MAIN, LAKE CITY, MI 48800__
(Insert address)

Amount of gift (In figures): $ __1,000__

Amount of gift (In words): __ONE THOUSAND AND $\frac{No}{100}$_____ dollars

George Edward Frisbie
Your Signature

Full name and address of person or charity to receive cash gift. (Name only one (1) person or charity here)

(Please print) _____
(Insert name)

of _____
(Insert address)

Amount of gift (In figures): $ _____

Amount of gift (In words): _____ dollars

Your Signature

This section of article 2 gives you the opportunity to make a maximum of two specific cash gifts to persons or organizations. As section 2.1 says, these cash gifts are completely optional. If you don't want to make any, leave the lines in section 2.1 blank.

If you think you want to make a cash gift, you must first understand how your gift will be paid from your estate. The payment of cash gifts has a fairly high priority during the distribution of an estate. As a result, cash gifts must be paid before some other property is distributed from your estate. Sometimes this can create a problem when an estate runs short of cash.

> *Example*: Edith has made a cash gift of $10,000 in her statutory will. After her death, Edith's estate has only $1,000 in cash and no other liquid assets. To raise cash to pay the cash gift, other property in the estate, which Edith wanted her children to share, might have to be sold or mortgaged.

As you can see, making cash gifts can affect, and sometimes even upset, a will's pattern of estate distribution. Consequently, before you make a cash gift—particularly a large one—consider what effect it might have on the distribution of your estate during probate.

You can name only one taker for each cash gift that you make. You cannot make shared cash gifts by naming two or more takers for a gift. What happens to a cash gift when its taker dies before you and is not around to take the gift?* It just so happens that Michigan has a law that says how such "frustrated" gifts shall be distributed. The fate of a frustrated cash gift in a statutory will depends on the identity of its deceased taker. When the deceased taker is your "close relative," the frustrated cash gift will go to his/her surviving children/descendants by "representation" (see Appendix A for who your close relatives are and what the representation pattern of distribution is). If the deceased taker is a remote relative (one who isn't a close relative), a nonrelative or an organization, the frustrated cash gift fails and the money will pass by section 2.3 of the will (see below for the pattern of distribution of property through section 2.3).

> *Example*: Edith makes a statutory will with cash gifts of $1,000 each to her daughter Shirley and her friend Phyllis. Later, Shirley and Phyllis die. Since Shirley was Edith's close relative, the cash gift to her will go to her daughter Rhonda instead. On the other hand, the cash gift to Phyllis will fail because she was not a close relative of Edith. The cash from that gift will pass through section 2.3 of Edith's statutory will.

If you want to make a cash gift, print the name and address of the taker on the top lines of the first cash gift portion of section 2.1. On the next two lines, write the amount of the gift in numbers and words. Sign your name on the line below that. If you want to make another cash gift, repeat this procedure in the second cash gift section of section 2.1.

---

* The same problem can happen when you have named an organization as the cash gift-taker and the organization is defunct at the time of your death.

2.2 PERSONAL AND HOUSEHOLD ITEMS.

I may leave a separate list or statement either in my handwriting or signed by me at the end, regarding gifts of specific books, jewelry, clothing, automobiles, furniture, and other personal and household items.

I give my spouse all my books, jewelry, clothing, automobiles, furniture, and other personal and household items not included on any such separate list or statement. If I am not married at the time I sign this will, or if my spouse dies before me, my personal representative shall distribute those items, as equally as possible, among my children who survive me. If no children survive me, these items shall be distributed as set forth in paragraph 2.3.

Any inheritance tax due shall be paid from the balance of my estate and not from these gifts.

Section 2.2

Section 2.2 distributes a willmaker's "personal and household items." The section defines these items as "books, jewelry, clothing, automobiles, furniture, and other personal and household items." Regrettably, the statutory will does not say what "other personal and household items" are. But they presumably include other miscellaneous things one might use or have around the house: dishes, utensils, appliances, tools, art objects, electronic equipment (televisions, stereos, personal computers, etc.) and recreational vehicles (bicycles, motorcycles, boats, etc.). Like other parts of a statutory will, section 2.2 makes a willmaker's spouse and children the preferred takers of these personal and household items. The chart below depicts the pattern of distribution for those items:

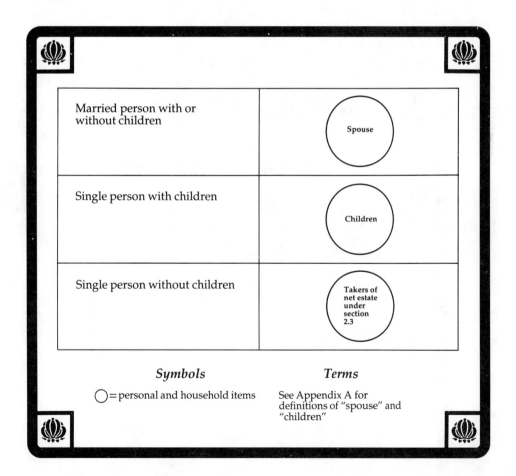

Married person with or without children	Spouse
Single person with children	Children
Single person without children	Takers of net estate under section 2.3

Symbols

◯ = personal and household items

Terms

See Appendix A for definitions of "spouse" and "children"

If you don't like this pattern, you can modify it by making a separate list to go along with your statutory will (see Appendix B for more on this). By making a separate list, you can give any of your personal and household items to your spouse and children in a different pattern, or give any of those items to other persons or organizations.

Example: George has two favorite guns. He wants to give one gun to his son Dewey and the other to his friend Ivan. George makes a separate list giving the guns to Dewey and Ivan. If George hadn't made these gifts in a separate list, section 2.2 of his statutory will would distribute the guns to Margo, or *all* his surviving children if Margo failed to survive him.

2.3 ALL OTHER ASSETS.

I give everything else I own to my spouse. If I am not married at the time I sign this will, or if my spouse dies before me, I give these assets to my children and the descendants of any deceased child. If no spouse, children, or descendants of children survive me, I choose <u>one</u> of the following distribution clauses by signing my name on the line after that clause. If I sign on both lines, or if I fail to sign on either line, or if I am not now married, these assets will go under distribution clause (b).

Section 2.3

Section 2.3 is really the heart of a statutory will because it distributes the willmaker's "net estate" (the statutory will calls this estate "all other assets"). In a statutory will, the net estate is what's left of the willmaker's estate after the deduction of: 1) charges against the estate (probate and funeral/burial expenses, debts, etc.) 2) any family rights 3) any specific gifts from a separate list or section 2.1 4) personal and household items from section 2.2 (when a spouse or children survive). Unless those deductions are large (which they usually aren't), the net estate will usually contain the bulk of a willmaker's estate. The chart below shows how a statutory will distributes the net estates of many willmakers:

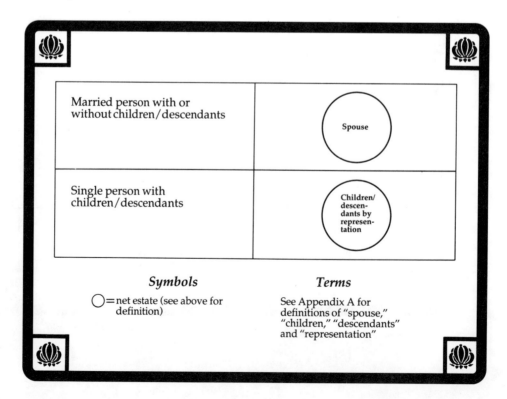

Married person with or without children/descendants	Spouse
Single person with children/descendants	Children/descendants by representation

Symbols

◯ = net estate (see above for definition)

Terms

See Appendix A for definitions of "spouse," "children," "descendants" and "representation"

According to section 2.3, married persons' net estates go to their spouses. The net estates of single persons with children/descendants go to their surviving children and descendants of any deceased children by representation. The representation pattern passes a deceased child's share along to her/her surviving children or descendants, who split it, usually equally, among themselves (see Appendix A for more about distributions by the representation pattern).

As you can see, the first part of section 2.3 creates a fairly comprehensive pattern of distribution for the net estates of married persons and those with children/descendants. By the same token, it does nothing for people who are single and have been childless. For them, the remaining part of section 2.3 will apply to pass their net estates.

2.3 ALL OTHER ASSETS.

I give everything else I own to my spouse. If I am not married at the time I sign this will, or if my spouse dies before me, I give these assets to my children and the descendants of any deceased child. If no spouse, children, or descendants of children survive me, I choose <u>one</u> of the following distribution clauses by signing my name on the line after that clause. If I sign on both lines, or if I fail to sign on either line, or if I am not now married, these assets will go under distribution clause (b).

Distribution clause, if no spouse, children, or descendants of children survive me (Select only one).

(a) One-half to be distributed to my heirs as if I did not have a will, and one-half to be distributed to my spouse's heirs as if my spouse had died just after me without a will.

George Edward Frisbie
(Your Signature)

(b) All to be distributed to my heirs as if I did not have a will.

_____
(Your Signature)

This part of section 2.3 distributes the net estates of persons who are single and have been childless. According to the terms of section 2.3(b), their net estates will be passed to their heirs as if they did not have a will. This pattern is simply the inheritance law pattern described in "Personalize Estate Distribution" in Chapter 1 and "Close Relatives and Heirs" in Appendix A. The statutory will adopts that pattern for single persons without children/descendants because it presumes that their heirs, as their closest family, would be the chosen takers of their net estates.

But besides distributing the net estates of persons who are single and have been childless, this part of section 2.3 has yet another important function. It distributes the net estates of other persons when their spouses and children/descendants have all failed to survive them. That possibility should be a particular worry of statutory willmakers like Thelma Frisbie (married, but with no children/descendants) and the adult Millsap children (either married or single with few children) because the death of their few close family members would leave them without net estate-takers. But dying without surviving close family can also be a concern for statutory willmakers with larger families—even those with several generations—because a common disaster could possibly wipe out their entire immediate families quickly.*

> *Example*: The Frisbie family is traveling in a car to a wedding when they get into a terrible automobile accident. The entire family dies together in the accident, leaving George and Margo with no surviving spouse or children/descendants to take their net estates.

A statutory will provides for the distribution of net estates in such cases in a general way, but with some flexibility. Section 2.3 gives you two choices for the distribution of your net estate when your spouse and children/descendants all fail to survive you:

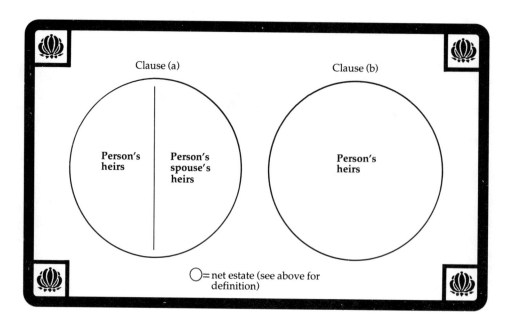

Single persons (with or without children/descendants) should select distribution clause (b) because clause (a) would not apply to them (since it divides the net estate with the heirs of one's *spouse*). On the other hand, married persons (with or without children/descendants) have a choice. They can: 1) divide the net estate among their and their spouse's heirs (clause (a)) 2) distribute the net estate to their heirs only (clause (b)). Of these two options, clause (a) might seem like an odd choice. After all, why would you

---

* A common disaster of that sort is less likely to happen to someone like Edith Millsap, who has a family of three generations living in different states, but it could conceivably happen even to her.

want to give your in-laws half your net estate? As it happens, there are some sound reasons for that particular distribution.

> *Example*: The Frisbies, who have not made wills, have been in the automobile accident described above. But in this scenario, Margo does not die right away. She lingers and dies one week after the accident. Because she survived everybody, Margo inherits George's and most of the rest of the family's estates. After her death, all this property goes to her brother Stu, her only relative, whom George and she always disliked. So the bulk of the Frisbies' wealth ends up on only one side of the family, with someone they disliked, to the exclusion of the Frisbie side of the family.

If the Frisbies had made statutory wills and selected clause (a), they could have avoided this distasteful distribution. Their choice of clause (a) would have resulted in the division of Margo's net estate into two equal shares, and the distribution of one share to her heirs (still Stu) and the other share to George's heirs. As in many cases like this, that distribution may be the fairer one.

Still, other people may not want to have their spouses' heirs share in the distribution of their net estates. Some people might have a genuine dislike for their in-laws and may not want to give them anything under any circumstances. In other cases, one's heirs may need the property more than one's in-laws, who might be well-off. For whatever reason, if you want to keep the distribution of your net estate among your heirs exclusively, select clause (b).

Married willmakers, who have a choice of either clause (a) or (b), should choose either by signing their names on the line immediately below the correct clause. Single willmakers should choose clause (b) by signing their names below that paragraph. (Single willmakers who select clause (a) by mistake will get clause (b) anyway.) If you sign below both paragraphs or fail to sign below either, clause (b) will be assigned to you by default.

ARTICLE 3. NOMINATIONS OF PERSONAL REPRESENTATIVE, GUARDIAN, AND CONSERVATOR

Personal representatives, guardians, and conservators have a great deal of responsibility. The role of a personal representative is to collect your assets, pay debts and taxes from those assets, and distribute the remaining assets as directed in the will. A guardian is a person who will look after the physical well-being of a child. A conservator is a person who will manage a child's assets and make payments from those assets for the child's benefit. Select them carefully. Also, before you select them, ask them whether they are willing and able to serve.

Article 3 of a statutory will is the place where you can appoint fiduciaries. Everyone will probably want to appoint personal representatives. If you have minor children, you will also want to appoint guardians and conservators for them. Finally, when you have legally incapacitated or developmentally disabled adult children, you may be able to appoint guardians for them as well (see "Appoint Fiduciaries" in Chapter 1 for more about this).

If you have reviewed Part II of this chapter, you should have already narrowed the field of fiduciary candidates to a few. But before you make your final selection, read the following sections about the specific qualifications for each type of fiduciary. On the basis of that information, you should select a first choice and substitute for each fiduciary you want to appoint. After you do that, insert the names and addresses of your fiduciary appointees in the appropriate lines in article 3.

3.1 PERSONAL REPRESENTATIVE. (Name at least one)

I nominate _MARGO ANN FRISBIE_
(Insert name of person or eligible financial institution)

of _900 E. WASHINGTON, LAKE CITY, MI 48800_
(Insert address)

to serve as personal representative.

If my first choice does not serve, I nominate

LAKE CITY BANK + TRUST
(Insert name of person or eligible financial institution)

of _101 S. MAIN, LAKE CITY, MI 48800_
(Insert address)

to serve as personal representative.

Section 3.1

You can appoint as your personal representative any person or financial institution legally eligible to serve as a fiduciary (see "Fiduciaries: Legal Eligibility" in Part II for more about these eligibility requirements). As explained in Chapter 1, the chief task of your personal representative is to probate your estate. A personal representative does not have to do that personally (s/he/it may hire a lawyer or others to handle the probate), but the personal representative must supervise the procedure. For that reason, a personal representative must be honest and reliable. Your personal representative doesn't necessarily have to possess any special expertise or training. Good judgment and common sense should be enough. However, in some cases, special skills might come in handy. For example, if you own a small business, you might want to appoint a personal representative who knows something about your business so that it could be operated during the probate of your estate.

Personal Representative

Your personal representative should be someone who is stable and likely to be around at your death. If your appointee is a person, s/he should be around your age, younger or otherwise in good health. As mentioned in Part II, persons who don't reside in Michigan can serve as personal representatives in this state. Nevertheless, nonresidents might find it difficult to supervise the probate of an estate long-distance. Because of that problem, you might want to give preference to Michigan residents.

When it comes to selecting personal representatives, some willmakers overlook their spouses. Yet spouses are often excellent choices as personal representatives. A spouse usually has all the practical qualities (honesty, availability, etc.) that you should seek in a fiduciary. What's more, it may be better to have the person who will take the estate probate it, because that person will have an incentive to do a good job. (Of course, spouses are the primary takers of married statutory willmakers' estates.) On the other hand, you are not compelled to select your spouse as your personal representative, and there certainly may be situations in which your spouse would be a poor choice.

3.2 GUARDIAN AND CONSERVATOR.

Your spouse may die before you. Therefore, if you have a child under age 18, name a person as guardian of the child, and a person or eligible financial institution as conservator of the child's assets. The guardian and the conservator may, but need not be, the same person.

If a guardian or conservator is needed for any child of mine, I nominate

CHESTER ARNOLD FRISBIE
(Insert name of person)

of 1601 S. MAPLE, LAKE CITY, MI 48800 as guardian
(Insert address)

and CHESTER ARNOLD FRISBIE
(Insert name of person or eligible financial institution)

of 1601 S. MAPLE, LAKE CITY, MI 48800
(Insert address)

as conservator.

If my first choice cannot serve, I nominate

WESLEY WALTER FRISBIE
(Insert name of person)

of 701 W. ELM, LAKE CITY, MI 48800 as guardian
(Insert address)

and ARCHIE LOUIS SAVAGE
(Insert name of person or eligible financial institution)

of 117 W. RIVER, LAKE CITY, MI 48800
(Insert address)

as conservator.

Section 3.2

Guardian and Conservator

Subject to several exceptions, most persons and financial institutions legally eligible to serve as fiduciaries can be appointed as guardians and conservators (see "Fiduciaries: Legal Eligibility" in Part II for more about these eligibility requirements). Your spouse should not be appointed for either position because your children will usually not need a guardian until your spouse is also deceased. Moreover, your surviving spouse will have a high priority to act as your children's conservator, if one is ever needed, even without an appointment from you. Eligible financial institutions can serve as conservators for your children. But they cannot act as guardians for them on account of one obvious reason: It's hardly possible for a financial institution to rear children!

There is nothing wrong with appointing the same person to act as both guardian and conservator for your children. As a matter of fact, the combination of those roles in one person often makes sense. When one person is simultaneously guardian and conservator, s/he would not have to apply to a separate conservator for funds to support their wards. Instead, the conservator-guardian would have the funds at hand to pay those costs as they are incurred. On the other hand, some people might not like such coziness. They might prefer to have different persons or institutions fill those positions so that they can check on each other.

Whether you select persons or institutions, you should choose your guardians and conservators carefully because their responsibilities are enormous. This is particularly true of guardians. The person you pick as guardian must have the ability and motivation to fulfill the role of parent to your children for what may be a number of years. In this regard, the selection of older persons, such as one's parents, might not be a good choice because they might not have the ability to rear children for a long period of time. Likewise, the appointment of young adults, such as the older brothers or sisters of minor children, might also be a poor choice since they often lack the maturity to act as parents for these children. Finally, if you appoint a guardian for your legally incapacitated or developmentally disabled child, the appointee must be able to provide for his/her special needs.

Although there are no legal barriers to appointing nonresident guardians, you must carefully consider the consequences of such an appointment. Ordinarily, wards will go to live with their guardians; guardians seldom move to live with their wards. This means that your children will probably have to move out of state, perhaps far away from their other family and friends, when their guardian is a nonresident. You must decide whether your children could adjust to a move like that.

A conservator, like a personal representative, is basically a manager of money and other property. Consequently, the practical qualifications for a conservator resemble those of a personal representative more than they do those of a guardian. Above all, your conservator appointees should possess good judgment and common sense. Financial or business expertise is not necessary, but it could be an advantage when a ward's estate is likely to be large or complex. As with personal representatives, you might want to consider selecting conservators who live near the wards and their estate property. Although nonresidents can serve as conservators, it might be difficult, as a practical matter, for a conservator to manage a ward's estate from a great distance.

You should always ask all fiduciary candidates about whether they are willing to serve before you actually appoint them. But obtaining such prior consent is especially important for guardian and conservator appointees because their responsibilities are so great. You should also discuss prospective guardian and conservator appointments with your teenage children because minor children 14 years of age or older have a say in guardian and conservator appointments for them. You see, children 14 years of age or older can object to the person appointed as guardian for them. After the objection, the probate judge must hold a hearing and appoint a suitable guardian for the child. Likewise, children 14 years of age or older have the right to nominate their own conservator candidates instead of their parents' appointees. When that happens, the probate judge must resolve the conflict when s/he appoints a conservator for the child. However, you can usually prevent such problems by discussing your prospective appointments with your teenage children and by appointing someone acceptable to them.

Coordinating Appointments

When you are married, you might also want to discuss your guardian and conservator appointments with your spouse. If you fail to do that, you and your spouse may end up appointing different appointees. At least in the case of guardian appointments, Michigan law says that the appointment in the will of the spouse/parent who dies last controls.

> *Example*: George and Margo make statutory wills. They thought they appointed the same persons as guardians of their children. However, they actually made different guardian appointments. George dies before Margo. Because Margo died last, the guardian appointments in her will are the ones that are effective.

> *Example*: Same as above except that George and Margo both die simultaneously in an airplane crash. Since neither of them died last, neither's guardian appointments have priority. What's worse, it turns out that both appointees want to be guardians of the children. They contest the issue in a guardianship proceeding in probate court.

To prevent these and similar problems, you and your spouse may want to coordinate your guardian and conservator appointments by appointing the same appointees. On the other hand, spouses don't have to coordinate their appointments unless they want to, and they could choose to appoint different guardians and conservators.

Guardian Appointments by Single Parents

Needless to say, single parents don't have to worry about coordinating their guardian and conservator appointments with spouses. However, some single parents may have another problem: whether their ex-spouses* will become guardians of their children after their deaths. Under old English will law, a father had the absolute right to appoint by will anybody he wanted as guardian of his children. By exercising that right, a father could even prevent the mother from getting custody of the children after his death. Nowadays, a surviving parent cannot be deprived of custody by a guardian appointment in the deceased parent's will. In fact, in most cases, the surviving parent automatically gets/keeps custody of the children when the other parent dies.

> *Example*: Shirley and her ex-husband Gus have gone through a bitter divorce in which Shirley got custody of their daughter Rhonda. She does not want Gus to regain custody of Rhonda after her death. Instead, she would like to name her brothers as Rhonda's guardians. But Shirley discovers that Gus, if he were to survive her, will get custody of Rhonda as her surviving parent. Resigning herself to that fact, she makes a statutory will and appoints Grover and Eugene as guardians for Rhonda.

---

*   Unwed parents may share this problem with other types of single parents.

Like Shirley, single parents should appoint the nonparents they want as guardians of their children. They must realize that these appointments will be effective after their deaths only if the other parent: 1) has also died 2) has been found to be legally incapacitated. Yet if the other parent survives and is in good health, s/he will get/keep custody of the children.* Moreover, the surviving parent can also determine the future custody of the children by making guardians appointments in his/her will (since the guardian appointments of the parent to die last prevail).** All of this shouldn't discourage single parents from making guardian appointments in their wills because, as you can see, their appointments can become effective in some cases. But it should deter a single parent from trying to use guardian appointments as a means of denying the other parent child custody after his/her death.

3.3 BOND.

A bond is a form of insurance in case your personal representative or a conservator performs improperly and jeopardizes your assets. A bond is not required. You may choose whether you wish to require your personal representative and any conservator to serve with or without bond. Bond premiums would be paid out of your assets.

(Select only one)

(a) My personal representative and any conservator I have named shall serve with bond.

_____
(Your signature)

(b) My personal representative and any conservator I have named shall serve without bond.

George Edward Frisbie
(Your signature)

Section 3.3 deals with bonds for personal representatives and conservators (guardians never give bonds because they don't handle much or any property). Bonds are promises by fiduciaries that they will pay losses they cause up to the amount of the bond. In some cases, these promises must also be guaranteed by bonding companies, which charge fees or premiums for the guarantee. When a bond is required, the probate judge will set the

---

*   As some consolation, Michigan law gives the parents of the deceased parent (the grandparents) the right to seek visitation with the grandchildren in these situations.

**   But if the surviving parent dies without having made guardian appointments in a will, the first deceased parent's guardian appointments will become effective.

amount of the bond. The bond amount may correspond to the value of the estate or it may be a nominal $1,000 amount.

Should you require your fiduciaries (your personal representatives and any conservators you have appointed) to post bonds? Ordinarily, you shouldn't need bonds for those fiduciaries if the persons you have appointed are honest. If they aren't, you shouldn't appoint them in the first place. Likewise, bonds are unnecessary when your appointees are financial institutions. By law, financial institutions eligible to serve as fiduciaries already have large bonds on deposit with the state treasurer to cover any losses they cause when they act as fiduciaries. Finally, any bond premiums must be paid from your or the wards' estates. When you waive bonds, you can save the cost of those premiums.

Section 3.3

Although section 3.3 gives you a choice about whether to require bonds of your fiduciaries, the probate judge, not you, actually has the final say-so about whether your fiduciaries must post bonds. However, you can state your wishes about the bond requirement here, which the judge must weigh when s/he decides the issue during probate. If you prefer bonds, sign your name on the line under clause (a). If you don't want bonds, sign your name under clause (b).

3.4 DEFINITIONS AND ADDITIONAL CLAUSES.

Definitions and additional clauses found at the end of this form are part of this will.

Definitions

The following definitions and rules of construction shall apply to this Michigan statutory will:

(a) "Assets" means all types of property you can own, such as real estate, stocks and bonds, bank accounts, business interests, furniture, and automobiles.

(b) "Jointly-held assets" means those assets ownership of which is transferred automatically upon the death of 1 of the owners to the remaining owner or owners.

(c) "Spouse" means your husband or wife at the time you sign this will.

(d) "Descendants" means your children, grandchildren, and their descendants.

(e) "Descendants" or "children" includes persons born or conceived during marriage, persons legally adopted, and persons born out of wedlock who would inherit if their parent died without a will.

(f) Whenever a distribution under a Michigan statutory will is to be made to a person's descendants, the assets are to be divided into as many equal shares as there are then living descendants of the nearest degree of living descendants and deceased descendants of that same degree who leave living descendants. Each living descendant of the nearest degree shall receive 1 share. The share of each deceased descendant of that same degree shall be divided among his or her descendants in the same manner.

(g) "Heirs" means those persons who would have received your assets if you had died without a will, domiciled in Michigan, under the laws which are then in effect.

(h) "Person" includes individuals and institutions.

(i) Plural and singular words include each other, where appropriate.

(j) If a Michigan statutory will states that a person shall perform an act, the person is required to perform that act. If a Michigan statutory will states that a person may do an act, the person's decision to do or not to do the act shall be made in a good faith exercise of the person's powers.

Additional Clauses

(a) Powers of personal representative.

(1) The personal representative shall have all powers of administration given by Michigan law to independent personal representatives, and the power to invest and reinvest the estate from time to time in any property, real or personal, even though such investment, by reason of its character, amount, proportion to the total estate, or otherwise, would not be considered appropriate for a fiduciary apart from this provision. In dividing and distributing the estate, the personal representative may distribute partially or totally in kind, may determine the value of distributions in kind without reference to income tax basis, and may make non pro rata distributions.

(2) The personal representative may distribute estate assets otherwise distributable to a minor beneficiary to (a) the conservator, or (b) in amounts not exceeding $5,000.00 per year, either to the minor, if married; to a parent or any adult person with whom the minor resides and who has the care, custody, or control of the minor; or the guardian. The personal representative is free of liability and is discharged from any further accountability for distributing assets in compliance with the provisions of this paragraph.

(b) Powers of guardian and conservator. A guardian named in this will shall have the same authority with respect to the child as a parent having legal custody would have. A conservator named in this will shall have all of the powers conferred by law.

Section 3.4

Section 3.4 makes the definitions and additional clauses that appear at the end of a statutory will part of the will. Most of these provisions have been covered in the preceding parts. But notice that the additional clauses section gives various powers to your fiduciaries with which they can carry out their duties. Basically, these provisions give your fiduciaries powers granted to them by statutory law, with a few more added in (a)(1) and (2) for good measure.

These provisions give your fiduciaries broad powers to do practically anything to perform their tasks. Some willmakers are uncomfortable about such broad grants of power and they may limit the powers of their fiduciaries in their wills. But most people believe that the better way is to select honest fiduciaries and give them broad powers to do their jobs. After all, if you mistrust your fiduciaries enough to restrict their powers, you probably shouldn't have chosen them anyway. This is the approach you must use with your statutory will, because you cannot change the broad powers that it gives to fiduciaries.

I sign my name to this Michigan statutory will on_____ , 19 _____ .

_____
(Your signature)

This is the final signature section where you will date and sign/acknowledge your statutory will before witnesses during the execution of the will. For now, you can leave this section blank.

NOTICE REGARDING WITNESSES

You must use two (2) adult witnesses who will not receive assets under this will. It is preferable to have three (3) adult witnesses. All the witnesses must observe you sign the will, or have you tell them you signed the will, or have you tell them the will was signed at your direction in your presence.

This notice gives you some general information about how your will must be executed. As the notice says, two but preferably three persons must witness the execution of your will. These witnesses must be adults who are "disinterested" in your will. Review "Selecting Witnesses for the Execution of Your Will" in Part II for more about witnesses. The instructions about the different will execution methods are covered in more detail in Part IV.

STATEMENT OF WITNESSES

We sign below as witnesses, declaring that the person who is making this will appears to be of sound mind and appears to be making this will freely and without duress, fraud, or undue influence and that the person making this will acknowledges that he or she has read, or has had it read to them, and understands the contents of this will.

_____	_____
(Print Name)	(Signature of Witness)
_____	
(Address)	
_____	
(City) (State) (Zip)	

_____	_____
(Print Name)	(Signature of Witness)
_____	
(Address)	
_____	
(City) (State) (Zip)	

_____	_____
(Print Name)	(Signature of Witness)
_____	
(Address)	
_____	
(City) (State) (Zip)	

This section is what lawyers call an "attestation clause." An attestation clause is a formal statement by the witnesses in which they say that they saw the willmaker's signing/acknowledgment of the will. In this particular attestation clause, the witnesses also say that the willmaker: 1) appeared to be of sound mind and free of duress, fraud or undue influence 2) acknowledged that s/he had read the will (or had it read to him/her) 3) and that s/he understood it. Including an attestation clause in a will is important because it can make the will easier to probate. Whatever its advantages, you should leave this section blank until you execute the will.

2

Part IV

Executing Your Statutory Will

*Copying
a Will*

Before you execute your statutory will, you should decide whether you want to make any photocopies of it. Your will is a private document. You don't have to show or give it to anyone else unless you want to. Even so, as explained below, there are several good reasons to make duplicate copies of your will to give to others or to keep for yourself.

By making copies of your will, you can keep a copy around the house, to review periodically, while the original will is stored in a more secure place. You may also want copies to give to your fiduciaries (some financial institutions may request copies when they have been appointed as fiduciaries). Finally, under some circumstances, a copy of a will can serve as a substitute for the original will when it has been lost or destroyed. Sometimes this can be the difference between dying with a will or without one. It certainly was for a woman who died in France in 1925. Her will had left her husband nothing. As the lawyer read the will, the irate husband snatched it from the lawyer's hands and ate it! Luckily, the lawyer had made a carbon copy of the will and it was probated in the original's place.

When you want to make copies of your will, make then now, before your will is executed. By having only copies of your will before execution, you make it slightly more difficult for someone to use a copy as the basis for a will contest against any subsequent will you may make later. But if you go to the trouble of making copies of your will, don't undo your work later by executing those copies during the execution of your will. When you execute your will, execute your original will only, leaving any copies you have made unexecuted.

Although you won't be needing your will copies during the execution of your will, don't distribute them to others just yet. As explained in Part V, you should add some information about the will execution to the copies of your will after the execution. Consequently, you should keep your copies around until then.

Finally, if you decide to make copies of your will, don't overdo it by making too many copies. When a will is replaced by a new will, the prior will *and all its copies* should be destroyed (see "Destroying Your Prior Wills" in Part V for more about this). If numerous copies of the prior will are in circulation, it might be difficult to collect and destroy them all. A copy of the repudiated will might survive and be used by someone in a will contest against the new will. Because of this risk, you should make copies of your will sparingly (perhaps two or three copies at the most).

Will Execution Methods

Michigan, like a lot of other states, used to have very complicated will execution requirements. Will executions had to follow a procedure in which those requirements were strictly observed. Because lawyers were the only ones who seemed to know this ritual, few people dared to make and execute wills by themselves. When Michigan will law was revised in 1979, will execution requirements were simplified. Nowadays, Michigan law provides for three fairly simple methods of will execution:

- signature by the willmaker before witnesses
- signature by proxy before witnesses
- previous signature of the will followed by the willmaker's acknowledgment of the signature (or the will) to witnesses

With each method, the will must be signed or acknowledged before two, but preferably three, "disinterested" witnesses (see "Selecting Witnesses for the Execution of Your Will" in Part II for more about the number and qualifications of witnesses). Some states have extra provisions for the execution of wills before notaries public or under oath. Michigan law does not provide for that sort of thing. In Michigan, the only persons you need for a will execution are your witnesses. As a matter of fact, besides your witnesses, it's best not to have any other persons present with you when you execute your will. The presence of others during will executions is not prohibited, but it could possibly raise questions of undue influence or duress by them.

Despite the flexibility of Michigan's will execution requirements, you must follow one very important rule during the execution of your will. The witnesses must be present with and actually observe you during the execution of your will by one of the three execution methods. Under no circumstances should the witnesses be absent or distracted during the execution procedure.

Signature before Witnesses

To sign before witnesses, a willmaker should gather with the witnesses in the same room and use the procedure described below. A portion of a sample will executed with this method is also reproduced below.

- The willmaker should tell the witnesses that s/he has read the will (or had it read to him/her) and that s/he understands it.

- The willmaker should date and sign the will in the final signature section.

- The willmaker should ask the witnesses to read the "Statement of Witnesses" and have them sign their names below that paragraph.

- The witnesses should also print their names and addresses on the lines to the left of their signatures.

I sign my name to this Michigan statutory will on _____ JANUARY 1 , 19 90 .

George Edward Frisbie
(Your signature)

NOTICE REGARDING WITNESSES

You must use two (2) adult witnesses who will not receive assets under this will. It is preferable to have three (3) adult witnesses. All the witnesses must observe you sign the will, or have you tell them you signed the will, or have you tell them the will was signed at your direction in your presence.

STATEMENT OF WITNESSES

We sign below as witnesses, declaring that the person who is making this will appears to be of sound mind and appears to be making this will freely and without duress, fraud, or undue influence and that the person making this will acknowledges that he or she has read, or has had it read to them, and understands the contents of this will.

ARCHIE LOUIS SAVAGE
(Print Name)

Archie Louis Savage
(Signature of Witness)

117 W. RIVER
(Address)

LAKE CITY   MI   48800
(City)   (State)   (Zip)

GUY FRANCIS FISH
(Print Name)

Guy Francis Fish
(Signature of Witness)

501 S STATE
(Address)

LAKE CITY   MI   48800
(City)   (State)   (Zip)

LUTHER ERNEST DOOLITTLE
(Print Name)

Luther Ernest Doolittle
(Signature of Witness)

222 N. LAKE
(Address)

LAKE CITY   MI   48800
(City)   (State)   (Zip)

Signature by Proxy

Michigan law also allows a willmaker to execute a will by having an authorized person, called a "proxy," make and/or sign the will on the willmaker's behalf. The procedure for making and executing a statutory will by proxy (with a sample proxy signature) is described below:

■ Before execution, the willmaker should direct the proxy during the completion of the title and articles of the will. Any signatures in articles 2 and 3 should be signed by the proxy on behalf of the willmaker as shown in the sample proxy signature below.

■ After the willmaker and proxy have made the will, they should gather with the witnesses in the same room.

■ The willmaker should tell the witnesses that s/he has read the will (or had it read to him/her) and that s/he understands it.

■ The willmaker should tell the witnesses that the proxy is signing the will on his/her behalf and at his/her direction.

■ The proxy should date and sign the will in the final signature section like the sample below:

George Edward Frizbie by Archie Louis Savage
AT THE FORMER'S DIRECTION AND IN HIS PRESENCE
_____
(Your signature)

■ The willmaker should ask the witnesses to read the "Statement of Witnesses" and have them sign their names below that paragraph.

■ The witnesses should also print their names and addresses on the lines to the left of their signatures.

When a willmaker is speechless, this procedure can be used with some modifications. Instead of receiving instructions from the willmaker, the proxy should ask the willmaker if s/he should do the things described above. For each question, the willmaker can give consent by nodding or otherwise signifying approval.

Acknowledgment of Previous Signature

A willmaker can sign a will personally or have it signed by proxy outside the presence of one or more of the witnesses and then acknowledge the signature to the absent witness(es) later. In that case, the will execution procedure would be as follows:

- The will shall have been previously dated and signed (by the willmaker personally or on his/her behalf by a proxy) in the final signature section (if this previous signature was before one or more witnesses, one of the other two execution methods should be used with respect to them, as in the execution by acknowledgment example below).

- The willmaker should then gather with the absent witness(es) in the same room and tell them that s/he has read the will (or had it read to him/her) and that s/he understands it.

- The willmaker should then point to the previous signature in the final signature section and tell the witnesses that it is his/her signature (if signed personally) or was made on his/her behalf (if signed by proxy).

- The willmaker should ask the witnesses to read the "Statement of Witnesses" and have them sign their names below that paragraph.

- The witnesses should also print their names and addresses on the lines to the left of their signatures.

Selecting a Will Execution Method

Despite having the choice of three will execution methods, the first (signature before witnesses) method is by far the safest method, and it should be used whenever possible. If you want to use either of the other two methods merely for the sake of convenience, you should postpone the execution of your will until the first method can be used instead. Nevertheless, under the right circumstances, the acknowledgment method of execution might have to be used.

> *Example*: George wants to execute his will quickly before he goes into the hospital for major surgery. He cannot get all three witnesses together at one time because one witness works a nightshift. He signs the will before the first two witnesses and then uses the second method of execution to acknowledge his previous signature before the absent third witness.

Finally, a willmaker who suffers from a physical disability might have to resort to the signature by proxy method. Naturally, the disability must be physical, not mental, because every willmaker must possess the proper mental capacity to make a will (see "Who Can Make a Statutory Will?" in Part II for more about this requirement).

> *Example*: George has been in an automobile accident and is paralyzed, although he is still mentally competent. He directs his proxy Archie during the making of the will and, with the witnesses looking on, asks Archie to sign the will for him.

21

Part V

After You Complete Your Statutory Will

After you execute your statutory will, staple the pages of the original will together to keep them from becoming separated in the future. If you have made duplicate copies of the will, staple their pages together as well. While you still have your original will and its copies together, you should also do two things to the copies: 1) print the date your will was signed in the dateline in the final signature sections of the copies (but don't sign these copies) 2) print the names and addresses of the witnesses who signed your will in the lines below the "Statement of Witnesses" sections of the copies. By adding this information, your copies, although unexecuted, will show the date of your will and who witnessed it. That information could come in handy later if your original will should ever become lost or destroyed and a copy has to substitute for it.

Destroying Your Prior Wills

When you make a statutory will, article 1 of the will provides that you "revoke any prior wills and codicils." Despite that provision, you should also revoke all your prior wills and codicils by destroying them along with all their copies. Some people hesitate to destroy their prior wills and they may wish to keep them around. But if you leave prior wills in circulation, you make it easier for someone to take a prior will of yours and propose it as your final will after your death. By destroying your prior wills and codicils, you make that practically impossible. Consequently, right after you execute your statutory will, collect your prior wills and codicils and all their copies. Destroy these documents by tearing them up and disposing of them in the trash.

Storing Your Will

In *The Pickwick Papers*, Charles Dickens tells of Susan Weller who left her will in a teapot for her husband Tony to find after her death. Unlike the careless Mrs. Weller, you mustn't be so casual about storing your will. On one hand, you should store your will in a place that is safe and secure during your lifetime. On the other hand, the place should be accessible to your survivors so they can get the will soon after your death. Mindful of that, willmakers usually choose one of the following places to store their wills:

Home safe. A safe located in your home is a good place to store your will if the safe is fireproof and waterproof. By storing your will at home, it should be readily accessible to your survivors after your death.

Safe deposit box. Many financial institutions and a few private storage companies have safe deposit boxes available that you can lease. A safe deposit box is a safe and secure place to store a will. But access to a safe deposit box after the box-holder's death can be difficult under some circumstances. When a safe deposit box has been leased by a box-holder alone, the box-holder's survivors must obtain the permission of either the probate court or the Michigan Department of Treasury to gain access to the box. This procedure might take awhile and delay the probate of the will.

Places for Will Storage

Access is easier when a safe deposit box has been leased jointly. In that case, the surviving box-holder has the right to remove the deceased box-holder's will or other papers from the box without obtaining any official permission. Consequently, when you want to store your will in a safe deposit box, you should consider leasing the box jointly with others, such as your spouse or children.

Vault at a financial institution. As a courtesy, some financial institutions will allow you to store your wills in their vaults, without charge, when you have appointed them as fiduciaries.

Probate court. You can also store your will in the probate court for the county in which your reside. When you store a will with a probate court, the court will keep it there until you choose to withdraw it or until your death. While the will is in storage, it is kept confidential and cannot be revealed to anyone.

Michigan probate courts charge a one-time fee of $5 for storage of a will. They also require that the will be submitted to them for storage in a sealed envelope or wrapper. The envelope or wrapper must also have written on it the willmaker's: 1) name 2) place of residence 3) social security number or driver's license number 4) date the will was submitted for storage 5) the name of the person who submitted it for storage.

Whichever storage method you use, it's important to tell your family and/or personal representative appointees where your will is located. When you have stored your will in a home safe or safe deposit box, you should also provide those people with keys to the safe or safe deposit box.

Distributing Will Copies

You don't have to store copies of your will as carefully as you have your original will. You may want to keep a copy of your will at home so that you can review it periodically to see if it needs revision. Sometimes a fiduciary, such as a personal representative, may want a copy of your will. Financial institutions may require copies for their files when they have been appointed as fiduciaries. But whenever you distribute copies of your will to others, keep track of where they are because you will want to be able to get them back to destroy if you decide to make a new will later.

Revising Your Will

The statutory will that you have made should reflect your current wishes about the distribution and settlement of your estate. Yet in the future your will may become obsolete and require revision. Wills may need to be revised for a number of reasons, but revision will be necessary most often when any one of the following events happens to you:

- your marriage, divorce, separation or the annulment of your marriage
- births or adoptions of children
- deaths of relatives or takers of your estate
- wish to change the pattern of estate distribution that your statutory will provides
- wish to change any of the fiduciary appointments you have made
- growth in the value of your wealth to a level that might result in significant death taxation
- your change of residence to another state

When any of these events happen, you should review your will to see if it should be revised. But above all, you must review your most carefully after you: 1) marry 2) end your marriage (by the death of your spouse, divorce or annulment), with or without a subsequent remarriage. As mentioned in Appendix A, a statutory will defines your spouse as the person whom you are legally married to *at the time you sign your statutory will*. If you are single when you make your statutory will, but marry later, your will might not recognize your new spouse.

> *Example*: Edith makes a statutory will. Later, she marries Reginald. Because Edith wasn't married to Reginald when she signed her statutory will, the will won't treat him as her spouse. If Edith were to die, Reginald would not get any distributions from sections 2.2 or 2.3 of her statutory will. Instead, he would receive a guaranteed marital share (in this case, whatever the inheritance law gives him), which might be less than what the statutory will would have given him.

Married statutory willmakers may encounter other problems when their marriages end (by the death of their spouses, divorce or annulment), regardless of whether they remarry afterward. If your spouse dies after you make a statutory will, it provides for alternate distributions of your estate to others (your children, descendants, etc.). Likewise, if you divorce or get an annulment after you make a will, Michigan law helpfully provides that: 1) all will distributions 2) any personal representative appointments in favor of your ex-spouse are automatically revoked. In that case, your estate will be distributed to others as if your ex-spouse had died before you. Despite those provisions, there still can be problems when married statutory willmakers change their marital status.

> *Example*: George makes a statutory will (like the one in Part III of Chapter 2). Later, he and Margo divorce. The divorce automatically revokes all will distributions to Margo and the appointment of her as personal representative. However, the divorce does not revoke any distributions to others. For instance, if George and his three children were to die in a common disaster, his estate might still be shared with his former in-laws according to section 2.3(a) of his will.

> Later, George remarries. As in the other example above, George's new wife would not be recognized by his statutory will. If George were to die, she, like Edith's new husband Reginald, would get only what her marital rights give her.

Because of these difficulties, both Edith and George should have reviewed and revised their wills after each significant change in their marital status. By the same token, minor changes in your personal situation might not require a revision of your will. For instance, if you were to change your residence to another Michigan county, or if your daughter's name changed after her marriage, you wouldn't necessarily have to revise your statutory will to mention those minor changes.

Will Revision

When revision of your statutory will is necessary, you mustn't attempt to do it by simply crossing out provisions or by inserting new ones. After a statutory will is executed, it is complete and must not be changed in any way. If you try to change your statutory will after you execute it, your modifications will be ineffective at best. At worst, they could result in the invalidation of the modified provisions or even the entire will!

One way to revise a will is to prepare a "codicil." A codicil is a will supplement that modifies the will in some way. Codicils must be written and they must be executed in the same manner as wills are (signed and usually witnessed). As a consequence, a codicil is usually about as much trouble to prepare as a new will. What's more, there is always a risk that a codicil will become lost or separated from the will that it modifies. If that happens, the codicil will be ineffective. Because of these problems, it's probably easiest and best to make a whole new will when you want to revise your statutory will. If a statutory will is still suitable for your needs, simply repeat the procedure described in this book and make a new statutory will.

Important Legal Terms

You may think that you know who your "spouse," "children" and "descendants" are, but these terms have precise legal meanings that may be a bit different from your notions. What's more, will and inheritance law have specialized terms like "heir" and "representation" with which you might not be familiar. All these terms are important because the inheritance law and a statutory will both use them in their estate distribution patterns. This appendix will help you understand the legal definitions of those terms.

Spouse

Your spouse is the person to whom you are *legally* married. Michigan allows two types of marriage: 1) ceremonial marriage (performed by most religious leaders and several types of government officials) 2) "secret marriage" (a rather obscure form of marriage performed by a probate judge for the benefit of: (a) people who have presented a good reason to keep their marriage secret (b) children under the age of 16 in certain circumstances). Common law marriage, in which persons informally agree to live together as man and wife, was abolished in Michigan after Jan. 1, 1957. However, Michigan residents who began living together as man and wife before that date might have a valid Michigan common law marriage. Michigan also recognizes all out-of-state marriages. So if a marriage were legal in the state where it began, it will be legal in Michigan. This recognition extends to common law marriages from the states that still permit them. As a result, persons who entered into common law marriages in those states will have legal marriages in Michigan. As of 1990, the District of Columbia and the following states permit common law marriages:

- Alabama
- Colorado
- Georgia
- Idaho
- Iowa
- Kansas
- Montana
- Ohio
- Oklahoma
- Pennsylvania
- Rhode Island
- South Carolina
- Texas

Even if you were married in one of those ways, your marriage could have already ended by divorce or annulment. Any divorce or annulment would have had to have been gotten from a court (there is no such thing as an informal "common law" divorce or annulment). If you suspect that you may have been a party to a divorce or annulment case, but don't know for sure, contact the divorce or annulment court's clerk to see whether a judgment was ever entered in the case. If you don't have much information about the divorce or annulment, check with a state vital statistics office for the state where you believe the divorce or annulment was obtained.* If a judgment of divorce or annulment was entered, that office should have a record of it.

Unlike a divorce or annulment, a separation will not end your marriage. If you are informally separated from your spouse (even while a divorce or annulment case is pending, but not yet finished), your marriage continues. Even a formal court-ordered "legal separation" (known as a "separate maintenance" in Michigan) will not sever the marital ties to your spouse.

Needless to say, the death of your spouse will also end your marriage. Nowadays, in an age of instant communications, you should know when your estranged spouse dies. Yet, there could be situations in which your spouse has completely disappeared and can be presumed dead. Michigan, like most states, has an "Enoch Arden" law (so called after the shipwrecked sailor of the Tennyson poem who returned from ten years at sea to find his wife remarried) that allows a person to be presumed dead after seven years of complete absence.

Although the inheritance law and a statutory will use those principles in defining "spouse," they have slightly different definitions of that term. For the purposes of the inheritance law, your spouse is the person whom you are legally married to *at the time of your death*. By contrast, a statutory

---

*   In Michigan, that office is the Michigan Department of Public Health, Office of State Registrar, P.O. Box 30195, Lansing, MI 48909, (517) 335-8655. To locate the state vital statistics office in other states, obtain the booklet "Where to Write for Vital Records" (#167R), by sending $1.50 to: R. Woods, Consumer Information Center, P.O. Box 100, Pueblo, CO 81002.

After the Wedding, 1969

will defines your spouse as the person whom you are legally married to *at the time you sign your statutory will* (whose name appears in article 1 of your will). The difference between the two definitions is important, particularly for statutory willmakers. When single statutory willmakers marry after they make their wills, their new spouses will not be recognized as spouses by their statutory wills. As a consequence, the new spouses may not get any distributions from their spouses' statutory wills. Instead, they would have to rely on certain marital rights that Michigan law guarantees all spouses. Married statutory willmakers whose marriages end (by the death of their spouses, divorce or annulment) after they make their wills might encounter other distribution problems. What's more, formerly married statutory willmakers who remarry may face the problem of nonrecognition of their new spouses described above. For more about these difficulties, and solutions to them, see "Revising Your Will" in Part V of Chapter 2.

Children and Descendants

Your children are your offspring plus anyone you have adopted. Your descendants include your children, your children's children (grandchildren), your children's children's children (great-grandchildren), etc. The inheritance law has a standard definition of children that it uses in its patterns of estate distribution:

Your children		Comments
Children born or conceived during your marriage	Yes	But paternity can be disproved. If it is, the child will not be a child of the "father" unless he acknowledges paternity as described below
Children born to you out of wedlock (= illegitimate children)	Yes for woman No for man unless...	the man acknowledges paternity by: 1) written acknowledgment 2) correcting birth certificate 3) treating child as his
Children you have legally adopted	Yes	
Children given up for adoption or minor children over whom you have lost parental rights	No	
Your spouse's children from a previous marriage or relationship (= stepchildren)	No	But one can legally adopt stepchildren in a stepparent adoption
Foster children	No	

Although it doesn't come right out and say so, a statutory will adopts this standard definition of children. As a result, when you make a statutory will, your children/descendants will be automatically defined that way. For most people, that definition should be satisfactory. But some people might find the standard definition overbroad or too narrow.

Example: George has an out-of-wedlock child. After a blood test, George joins with the mother in acknowledging paternity in a written document. Despite that acknowledgment, George does not want his illegitimate child to share in any will distributions to his children/descendants.

Example: If Grover were to make a statutory will, any distributions from his will to his children would go to all four of his children, including Garth, his child from his previous marriage. If Grover's wife Doreen were to make a statutory will, any distributions from her will to her children would go only to the three children she and Grover had (Garth would be excluded since he is Doreen's step-child).

If Grover were to die, Doreen would get his estate. When she dies, her estate (which, by now, includes Grover's probate and probably nonprobate property) will go to her three children only, leaving Garth with nothing.

In these examples, statutory wills might be unsuitable because of the way they define children. George may want to make an ordinary or holographic will in which he could redefine his children to exclude his illegitimate child. If Grover were worried about a possible disinheritance of Garth, he might consider making a large cash gift to him in a statutory will and/or giving other personal property to him in a separate list outside a statutory will. But probably the better solution would be for Grover to make an ordinary or holographic will and either: 1) set aside a portion of his estate in a trust for Garth 2) have Doreen and him make will gifts to Garth and contractually agree not to modify them.

Close Relatives and Heirs

According to some inheritance laws, any blood relative of a deceased person is eligible to inherit from him/her. Under these schemes, a very remote relative—such as a second or third cousin—can sometimes inherit when a deceased left no closer relatives. This sort of heir is sometimes called a "laughing heir," presumably because the heir must be amused when s/he inherits property from someone s/he scarcely or never knew. Michigan's inheritance law attempts to eliminate laughing heirs by restricting inheritance to certain "close relatives." These close relatives include your:

- children and descendants (grandchildren, great-grandchildren, etc.)
- parents
- brothers/sisters and their children (nephews/nieces)
- grandparents and their descendants (uncles/aunts, first cousins, first cousins once-removed, etc.)

Your heirs are drawn from those close relatives and one relative-by-marriage: your spouse. At your death, the surviving members of the group of these relatives that is most closely related to you (closeness of relation is defined by the inheritance law, as shown below) become your heirs. Otherwise, your more distant relatives do not qualify as your heirs (although, as explained below, this rule is bent a bit when representation is called for). The chart below depicts how the inheritance law determines heirs and their shares:

Married person with children/descendants when all children are also children of spouse (= surviving spouse has no stepchildren)	Spouse + Spouse | Children/descendants by representation
Married person with children/descendants when some children are not children of spouse (= surviving spouse has stepchildren)	Spouse | Children/descendants by representation
Married person without children/descendants, but with parents	Spouse + Spouse | Parents
Married person without children/descendants or parents	Spouse
Single person with children/descendants	Children/descendants by representation
Single person without children/descendants, but with parents	Parents
Single person without children/descendants or parents, but with brothers or sisters/their children	Brothers and sisters/their children by representation
Single person, no children/descendants, parents, brothers or sisters/their children, but with grandparents/their descendants	Maternal grandparents/their descendants by representation* | Paternal grandparents/their descendants by representation*
Single person with none of the above relatives	State of Michigan

Symbols

☐ = first $60,000 of net estate

◯ = 1) any remainder of net estate if $60,000 has been deducted for the spouse 2) otherwise, entire net estate

Terms

Net estate = probate estate after charges against estate and any family rights have been deducted

See Appendix A for definitions of "spouse," "children," "descendants" and "representation"

Notes

* If one side of the family fails, the other side takes all

Representation

Representation is a pattern of estate distribution that the inheritance law uses to pass the shares of some deceased would-be heirs on to their children/descendants. A statutory will also uses the representation pattern to dispose of cash gifts and net estates in some cases (see Part III in Chapter 2 for more about this).* When it applies, representation permits a deceased person's surviving children/descendants to stand in or "represent" him/her in the distribution pattern (hence the name). In that case, the deceased's surviving children/descendants take the share and divide it, usually equally, among themselves. The following examples show how representation works in practice:

> *Example*: Edith dies preceded in death by Grover. At Edith's death, Grover was survived by his wife Doreen and four children. According to representation, Grover's four children (Edith's grandchildren (= GC)) would represent him in the distribution pattern and take his one-fourth share to divide equally among themselves.

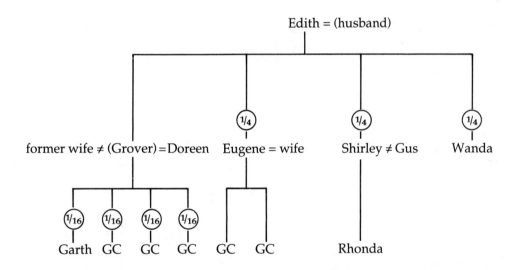

> *Example*: In this case, Grover, Shirley and Wanda have all died before Edith. The death of Wanda, without children/descendants, has the effect of increasing the amount of the shares for the other takers.

---

* A statutory will does not actually use the term "representation" in those situations, but that is the type of distribution provided for in definition (f) at the end of the will.

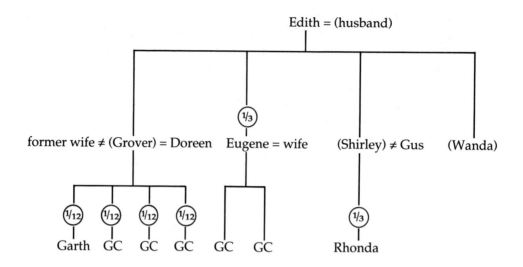

Example: In this scenario, all of Edith's children have died before her. Ordinarily, the surviving grandchildren would take and divide their parents' shares. But because there are only grandchildren, the share-division occurs at their level, giving them equal shares in this case.

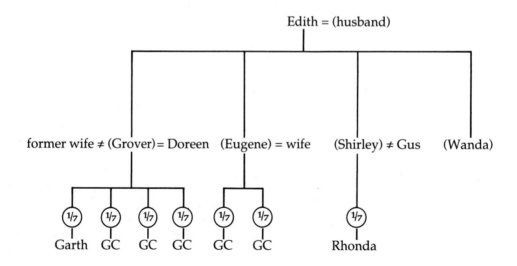

Appendix B

Making a Separate List

Michigan law permits willmakers to transfer certain types of property outside their wills in separate lists. According to section 2.2 of a statutory will, statutory willmakers can use these lists to dispose of their "personal and household items." These items include "specific books, jewelry, clothing, automobiles, furniture, and other personal and household items" (see the paragraph below section 2.2 in Part III of Chapter 2 for more about what miscellaneous personal and household items might include).

As a matter of fact, separate lists are particularly useful for statutory willmakers because they can use them to modify the pattern by which a statutory will distributes their personal and household items. You will recall that section 2.2 of a statutory will passes those items to one's spouse, children or those taking the net estate, in that order. If you make a separate list, you can modify that pattern and give any of your personal and household items to your spouse and children in a different pattern, or give any of those items to other persons or organizations.

> *Example*: George has two favorite guns. He wants to give one gun to his son Dewey and the other to his friend Ivan. George makes a separate list giving the guns to Dewey and Ivan. If George hadn't made these gifts in a separate list, section 2.2 of his statutory will would distribute the guns to Margo, or *all* his surviving children if Margo failed to survive him.

Preparing a Separate List

When you dispose of property in a separate list, you are making a sort of specific gift. See "Specific Gifts" in Part II of Chapter 2 for more about which persons and organizations can take specific gifts and how to identify those gift-takers. Besides those rules, you should also observe the rules listed below when you make any gifts in a separate list. A sample separate list is also included below to show you how to make a separate list using one of the forms from the end of this book (two separate list forms are included for married couples).

SEPARATE LIST

for the Michigan statutory will of

GEORGE EDWARD FRISBIE
_____
(Full name)

According to section 2.2 of my Michigan statutory will and section 131a of the Revised Probate Code of Michigan, I give the following personal and household items to the persons designated below:

WESTMINSTER MODEL 700 .17-CALIBER RIFLE TO DEWEY DONALD FRISBIE, 900 E. WASHINGTON, LAKE CITY, MI 48800

SMITH AND JAMES 1955 MODEL 25 .22-CALIBER REVOLVER TO IVAN EDGAR GOOCH, 279 W. CHERRY, LAKE CITY, MI 48800

I sign my name to this separate list on _____ JANUARY 1, 19 90 .

George Edward Frisbie
(Signature)

- Use a typewriter or pen with dark permanent ink to make your separate list. Never use a pencil or a pen with erasable ink.

- Your separate list can be printed (by hand or typewriter) or written. All the provisions must be legible, so if your writing is bad you might want to consider printing instead.

- The items you give must be described in enough detail so that your personal representative can identify them after your death. Any distinctive characteristics, marks or identification numbers should be mentioned in the gift of the item.

- Avoid shared gifts in which one item is given to two or more takers.

- The gifts should be clear and direct without any "strings" or conditions.

- You must date and sign the list at the end. It does not have to be witnessed or notarized.

- If you can't fit all your gifts on the one-page separate list form provided, you can add extra pages (using blank paper) to the form. However, if you do that, make sure that you: 1) number all the pages 2) date and sign *the last page* of your list *below its final provision* 3) staple all the pages of the list together.

After You Make a Separate List

You may want to make photocopies of your separate list to go with any copies of your will that you have made. You should store your original separate list with your original will (and copies of your separate list with copies of your will) because the two documents must be read and interpreted together after your death.

Unlike a statutory will, which must not be changed after it has been executed, a separate list can be revised freely. If you want to change any provisions in your separate list, you can simply strike them out and/or add new ones. When you revise your separate list that way, make sure that the strike-throughs are done neatly and completely. However, you may want to make a completely new separate list when your revisions are extensive because a severely edited document may be hard to read. If you make a new separate list, destroy the old one and its copies, and store the new list with your original will as described above.

MICHIGAN STATUTORY WILL

NOTICE

1. Any person age 18 or older and of sound mind may sign a will.
2. There are several kinds of wills. If you choose to complete this form, you will have a Michigan statutory will. If this will does not meet your wishes in any way, you should talk with a lawyer before choosing a Michigan statutory will.
3. Warning! It is strongly recommended that you do not add or cross out any words on this form except for filling in the blanks because all or part of this will may not be valid if you do so.
4. This will has no effect on jointly-held assets, on retirement plan benefits, or on life insurance on your life if you have named a beneficiary who survives you.
5. This will is not designed to reduce inheritance or estate taxes.
6. This will treats adopted children and children born outside of wedlock who would inherit if their parent died without a will the same way as children born or conceived during marriage.
7. You should keep this will in your safe deposit box or other safe place. By paying a small fee, you may file the will in your county's probate court for safekeeping. You should tell your family where the will is kept.
8. You may make and sign a new will at any time. If you marry or divorce after you sign this will, you should make and sign a new will.

INSTRUCTIONS:

1. To have a Michigan statutory will, you must complete the blanks on the will form. You may do this yourself, or direct someone to do it for you. You must either sign the will or direct someone else to sign it in your name and in your presence.
2. Read the entire Michigan statutory will carefully before you begin filling in the blanks. If there is anything you do not understand, you should ask a lawyer to explain it to you.

MICHIGAN STATUTORY WILL

of

_____
(Print or type your full name)

ARTICLE 1. DECLARATIONS

This is my will and I revoke any prior wills and codicils. I live in _____ County, Michigan.

My spouse is _____
(Insert spouse's name or write "None")

My children now living are:

_____   _____
(Insert names or write "None")

_____   _____

_____   _____

ARTICLE 2. DISPOSITION OF MY ASSETS

2.1 CASH GIFTS TO PERSONS OR CHARITIES. (Optional)

I can leave no more than two (2) cash gifts. I make the following cash gifts to the persons or charities in the amounts stated here. Any inheritance tax due shall be paid from the balance of my estate and not from these gifts.

Full name and address of person or charity to receive cash gift. (Name only one (1) person or charity here) (Please print) _____
(Insert name)

of _____
(Insert address)

Amount of gift (In figures): $ _____

Amount of gift (In words): _____ dollars

_____
Your Signature

Full name and address of person or charity to receive cash gift. (Name only one (1) person or charity here) (Please print) _____
(Insert name)

of _____
(Insert address)

Amount of gift (In figures): $ _____

Amount of gift (In words): _____ dollars

_____
Your Signature

2.2 PERSONAL AND HOUSEHOLD ITEMS.

I may leave a separate list or statement either in my handwriting or signed by me at the end, regarding gifts of specific books, jewelry, clothing, automobiles, furniture, and other personal and household items.

I give my spouse all my books, jewelry, clothing, automobiles, furniture, and other personal and household items not included on any such separate list or statement. If I am not married at the time I sign this will, or if my spouse dies before me, my personal representative shall distribute those items, as equally as possible, among my children who survive me. If no children survive me, these items shall be distributed as set forth in paragraph 2.3.

Any inheritance tax due shall be paid from the balance of my estate and not from these gifts.

2.3 ALL OTHER ASSETS.

I give everything else I own to my spouse. If I am not married at the time I sign this will, or if my spouse dies before me, I give these assets to my children and the descendants of any deceased child. If no spouse, children, or descendants of children survive me, I choose one of the following distribution clauses by signing my name on the line after that clause. If I sign on both lines, or if I fail to sign on either line, or if I am not now married, these assets will go under distribution clause (b).

Distribution clause, if no spouse, children, or descendants of children survive me (Select only one).

(a) One-half to be distributed to my heirs as if I did not have a will, and one-half to be distributed to my spouse's heirs as if my spouse had died just after me without a will.

_____
(Your Signature)

(b) All to be distributed to my heirs as if I did not have a will.

_____
(Your Signature)

ARTICLE 3. NOMINATIONS OF PERSONAL REPRESENTATIVE, GUARDIAN, AND CONSERVATOR

Personal representatives, guardians, and conservators have a great deal of responsibility. The role of a personal representative is to collect your assets, pay debts and taxes from those assets, and distribute the remaining assets as directed in the will. A guardian is a person who will look after the physical well-being of a child. A conservator is a person who will manage a child's assets and make payments from those assets for the child's benefit. Select them carefully. Also, before you select them, ask them whether they are willing and able to serve.

3.1 PERSONAL REPRESENTATIVE. (Name at least one)

I nominate _____
(Insert name of person or eligible financial institution)

of _____
(Insert address)

to serve as personal representative.

If my first choice does not serve, I nominate

_____
(Insert name of person or eligible financial institution)

of _____
(Insert address)

to serve as personal representative.

3.2 GUARDIAN AND CONSERVATOR.

Your spouse may die before you. Therefore, if you have a child under age 18, name a person as guardian of the child, and a person or eligible financial institution as conservator of the child's assets. The guardian and the conservator may, but need not be, the same person.

If a guardian or conservator is needed for any child of mine, I nominate

_____
(Insert name of person)

of _____ as guardian
(Insert address)

and _____
(Insert name of person or eligible financial institution)

of _____
(Insert address)

as conservator.

If my first choice cannot serve, I nominate

_____
(Insert name of person)

of _____ as guardian
(Insert address)

and _____
(Insert name of person or eligible financial institution)

of _____
(Insert address)

as conservator.

3.3 BOND.

A bond is a form of insurance in case your personal representative or a conservator performs improperly and jeopardizes your assets. A bond is not required. You may choose whether you wish to require your personal representative and any conservator to serve with or without bond. Bond premiums would be paid out of your assets.

(Select only one)

(a) My personal representative and any conservator I have named shall serve with bond.

_____
(Your signature)

(b) My personal representative and any conservator I have named shall serve without bond.

_____
(Your signature)

3.4 DEFINITIONS AND ADDITIONAL CLAUSES.

Definitions and additional clauses found at the end of this form are part of this will.

I sign my name to this Michigan statutory will on_____ , 19 _____.

_____
(Your signature)

NOTICE REGARDING WITNESSES

You must use two (2) adult witnesses who will not receive assets under this will. It is preferable to have three (3) adult witnesses. All the witnesses must observe you sign the will, or have you tell them you signed the will, or have you tell them the will was signed at your direction in your presence.

STATEMENT OF WITNESSES

We sign below as witnesses, declaring that the person who is making this will appears to be of sound mind and appears to be making this will freely and without duress, fraud, or undue influence and that the person making this will acknowledges that he or she has read, or has had it read to them, and understands the contents of this will.

_____   _____
(Print Name)   (Signature of Witness)

_____
(Address)

_____
(City)   (State)   (Zip)

_____   _____
(Print Name)   (Signature of Witness)

_____
(Address)

_____
(City)   (State)   (Zip)

_____   _____
(Print Name)   (Signature of Witness)

_____
(Address)

_____
(City)   (State)   (Zip)

Definitions

The following definitions and rules of construction shall apply to this Michigan statutory will:

(a) "Assets" means all types of property you can own, such as real estate, stocks and bonds, bank accounts, business interests, furniture, and automobiles.

(b) "Jointly-held assets" means those assets ownership of which is transferred automatically upon the death of 1 of the owners to the remaining owner or owners.

(c) "Spouse" means your husband or wife at the time you sign this will.

(d) "Descendants" means your children, grandchildren, and their descendants.

(e) "Descendants" or "children" includes persons born or conceived during marriage, persons legally adopted, and persons born out of wedlock who would inherit if their parent died without a will.

(f) Whenever a distribution under a Michigan statutory will is to be made to a person's descendants, the assets are to be divided into as many equal shares as there are then living descendants of the nearest degree of living descendants and deceased descendants of that same degree who leave living descendants. Each living descendant of the nearest degree shall receive 1 share. The share of each deceased descendant of that same degree shall be divided among his or her descendants in the same manner.

(g) "Heirs" means those persons who would have received your assets if you had died without a will, domiciled in Michigan, under the laws which are then in effect.

(h) "Person" includes individuals and institutions.

(i) Plural and singular words include each other, where appropriate.

(j) If a Michigan statutory will states that a person shall perform an act, the person is required to perform that act. If a Michigan statutory will states that a person may do an act, the person's decision to do or not to do the act shall be made in a good faith exercise of the person's powers.

Additional Clauses

(a) Powers of personal representative.

(1) The personal representative shall have all powers of administration given by Michigan law to independent personal representatives, and the power to invest and reinvest the estate from time to time in any property, real or personal, even though such investment, by reason of its character, amount, proportion to the total estate, or otherwise, would not be considered appropriate for a fiduciary apart from this provision. In dividing and distributing the estate, the personal representative may distribute partially or totally in kind, may determine the value of distributions in kind without reference to income tax basis, and may make non pro rata distributions.

(2) The personal representative may distribute estate assets otherwise distributable to a minor beneficiary to (a) the conservator, or (b) in amounts not exceeding $5,000.00 per year, either to the minor, if married; to a parent or any adult person with whom the minor resides and who has the care, custody, or control of the minor; or the guardian. The personal representative is free of liability and is discharged from any further accountability for distributing assets in compliance with the provisions of this paragraph.

(b) Powers of guardian and conservator. A guardian named in this will shall have the same authority with respect to the child as a parent having legal custody would have. A conservator named in this will shall have all of the powers conferred by law.

MICHIGAN STATUTORY WILL

NOTICE

1. Any person age 18 or older and of sound mind may sign a will.
2. There are several kinds of wills. If you choose to complete this form, you will have a Michigan statutory will. If this will does not meet your wishes in any way, you should talk with a lawyer before choosing a Michigan statutory will.
3. Warning! It is strongly recommended that you do not add or cross out any words on this form except for filling in the blanks because all or part of this will may not be valid if you do so.
4. This will has no effect on jointly-held assets, on retirement plan benefits, or on life insurance on your life if you have named a beneficiary who survives you.
5. This will is not designed to reduce inheritance or estate taxes.
6. This will treats adopted children and children born outside of wedlock who would inherit if their parent died without a will the same way as children born or conceived during marriage.
7. You should keep this will in your safe deposit box or other safe place. By paying a small fee, you may file the will in your county's probate court for safekeeping. You should tell your family where the will is kept.
8. You may make and sign a new will at any time. If you marry or divorce after you sign this will, you should make and sign a new will.

INSTRUCTIONS:

1. To have a Michigan statutory will, you must complete the blanks on the will form. You may do this yourself, or direct someone to do it for you. You must either sign the will or direct someone else to sign it in your name and in your presence.
2. Read the entire Michigan statutory will carefully before you begin filling in the blanks. If there is anything you do not understand, you should ask a lawyer to explain it to you.

MICHIGAN STATUTORY WILL

of

_____
(Print or type your full name)

ARTICLE 1. DECLARATIONS

This is my will and I revoke any prior wills and codicils. I live in _____ County, Michigan.

My spouse is _____
(Insert spouse's name or write "None")

My children now living are:

_____   _____
(Insert names or write "None")

_____   _____

_____   _____

ARTICLE 2. DISPOSITION OF MY ASSETS

2.1 CASH GIFTS TO PERSONS OR CHARITIES. (Optional)

I can leave no more than two (2) cash gifts. I make the following cash gifts to the persons or charities in the amounts stated here. Any inheritance tax due shall be paid from the balance of my estate and not from these gifts.

Full name and address of person or charity to receive cash gift. (Name only one (1) person or charity here)
(Please print) _____
(Insert name)

of _____
(Insert address)

Amount of gift (In figures): $ _____

Amount of gift (In words): _____ dollars

_____
Your Signature

Full name and address of person or charity to receive cash gift. (Name only one (1) person or charity here)
(Please print) _____
(Insert name)

of _____
(Insert address)

Amount of gift (In figures): $ _____

Amount of gift (In words): _____ dollars

_____
Your Signature

2.2 PERSONAL AND HOUSEHOLD ITEMS.

I may leave a separate list or statement either in my handwriting or signed by me at the end, regarding gifts of specific books, jewelry, clothing, automobiles, furniture, and other personal and household items.

I give my spouse all my books, jewelry, clothing, automobiles, furniture, and other personal and household items not included on any such separate list or statement. If I am not married at the time I sign this will, or if my spouse dies before me, my personal representative shall distribute those items, as equally as possible, among my children who survive me. If no children survive me, these items shall be distributed as set forth in paragraph 2.3.

Any inheritance tax due shall be paid from the balance of my estate and not from these gifts.

2.3 ALL OTHER ASSETS.

I give everything else I own to my spouse. If I am not married at the time I sign this will, or if my spouse dies before me, I give these assets to my children and the descendants of any deceased child. If no spouse, children, or descendants of children survive me, I choose <u>one</u> of the following distribution clauses by signing my name on the line after that clause. If I sign on both lines, or if I fail to sign on either line, or if I am not now married, these assets will go under distribution clause (b).

Distribution clause, if no spouse, children, or descendants of children survive me (Select only one).

(a) One-half to be distributed to my heirs as if I did not have a will, and one-half to be distributed to my spouse's heirs as if my spouse had died just after me without a will.

_____
(Your Signature)

(b) All to be distributed to my heirs as if I did not have a will.

_____
(Your Signature)

ARTICLE 3. NOMINATIONS OF PERSONAL REPRESENTATIVE, GUARDIAN, AND CONSERVATOR

Personal representatives, guardians, and conservators have a great deal of responsibility. The role of a personal representative is to collect your assets, pay debts and taxes from those assets, and distribute the remaining assets as directed in the will. A guardian is a person who will look after the physical well-being of a child. A conservator is a person who will manage a child's assets and make payments from those assets for the child's benefit. Select them carefully. Also, before you select them, ask them whether they are willing and able to serve.

3.1 PERSONAL REPRESENTATIVE. (Name at least one)

I nominate _____
(Insert name of person or eligible financial institution)

of _____
(Insert address)

to serve as personal representative.

If my first choice does not serve, I nominate

_____
(Insert name of person or eligible financial institution)

of _____
(Insert address)

to serve as personal representative.

3.2 GUARDIAN AND CONSERVATOR.

Your spouse may die before you. Therefore, if you have a child under age 18, name a person as guardian of the child, and a person or eligible financial institution as conservator of the child's assets. The guardian and the conservator may, but need not be, the same person.

If a guardian or conservator is needed for any child of mine, I nominate

_____
(Insert name of person)

of _____ as guardian
(Insert address)

and _____
(Insert name of person or eligible financial institution)

of _____
(Insert address)

as conservator.

If my first choice cannot serve, I nominate

_____
(Insert name of person)

of _____ as guardian
(Insert address)

and _____
(Insert name of person or eligible financial institution)

of _____
(Insert address)

as conservator.

3.3 BOND.

A bond is a form of insurance in case your personal representative or a conservator performs improperly and jeopardizes your assets. A bond is not required. You may choose whether you wish to require your personal representative and any conservator to serve with or without bond. Bond premiums would be paid out of your assets.

(Select only one)

(a) My personal representative and any conservator I have named shall serve with bond.

_____
(Your signature)

(b) My personal representative and any conservator I have named shall serve without bond.

_____
(Your signature)

3.4 DEFINITIONS AND ADDITIONAL CLAUSES.

Definitions and additional clauses found at the end of this form are part of this will.

I sign my name to this Michigan statutory will on_____, 19 _____.

_____
(Your signature)

NOTICE REGARDING WITNESSES

You must use two (2) adult witnesses who will not receive assets under this will. It is preferable to have three (3) adult witnesses. All the witnesses must observe you sign the will, or have you tell them you signed the will, or have you tell them the will was signed at your direction in your presence.

STATEMENT OF WITNESSES

We sign below as witnesses, declaring that the person who is making this will appears to be of sound mind and appears to be making this will freely and without duress, fraud, or undue influence and that the person making this will acknowledges that he or she has read, or has had it read to them, and understands the contents of this will.

_____   _____
(Print Name)   (Signature of Witness)

_____
(Address)

_____
(City)   (State)   (Zip)

_____   _____
(Print Name)   (Signature of Witness)

_____
(Address)

_____
(City)   (State)   (Zip)

_____   _____
(Print Name)   (Signature of Witness)

_____
(Address)

_____
(City)   (State)   (Zip)

Definitions

The following definitions and rules of construction shall apply to this Michigan statutory will:

(a) "Assets" means all types of property you can own, such as real estate, stocks and bonds, bank accounts, business interests, furniture, and automobiles.

(b) "Jointly-held assets" means those assets ownership of which is transferred automatically upon the death of 1 of the owners to the remaining owner or owners.

(c) "Spouse" means your husband or wife at the time you sign this will.

(d) "Descendants" means your children, grandchildren, and their descendants.

(e) "Descendants" or "children" includes persons born or conceived during marriage, persons legally adopted, and persons born out of wedlock who would inherit if their parent died without a will.

(f) Whenever a distribution under a Michigan statutory will is to be made to a person's descendants, the assets are to be divided into as many equal shares as there are then living descendants of the nearest degree of living descendants and deceased descendants of that same degree who leave living descendants. Each living descendant of the nearest degree shall receive 1 share. The share of each deceased descendant of that same degree shall be divided among his or her descendants in the same manner.

(g) "Heirs" means those persons who would have received your assets if you had died without a will, domiciled in Michigan, under the laws which are then in effect.

(h) "Person" includes individuals and institutions.

(i) Plural and singular words include each other, where appropriate.

(j) If a Michigan statutory will states that a person shall perform an act, the person is required to perform that act. If a Michigan statutory will states that a person may do an act, the person's decision to do or not to do the act shall be made in a good faith exercise of the person's powers.

Additional Clauses

(a) Powers of personal representative.

(1) The personal representative shall have all powers of administration given by Michigan law to independent personal representatives, and the power to invest and reinvest the estate from time to time in any property, real or personal, even though such investment, by reason of its character, amount, proportion to the total estate, or otherwise, would not be considered appropriate for a fiduciary apart from this provision. In dividing and distributing the estate, the personal representative may distribute partially or totally in kind, may determine the value of distributions in kind without reference to income tax basis, and may make non pro rata distributions.

(2) The personal representative may distribute estate assets otherwise distributable to a minor beneficiary to (a) the conservator, or (b) in amounts not exceeding $5,000.00 per year, either to the minor, if married; to a parent or any adult person with whom the minor resides and who has the care, custody, or control of the minor; or the guardian. The personal representative is free of liability and is discharged from any further accountability for distributing assets in compliance with the provisions of this paragraph.

(b) Powers of guardian and conservator. A guardian named in this will shall have the same authority with respect to the child as a parent having legal custody would have. A conservator named in this will shall have all of the powers conferred by law.

SEPARATE LIST

for the Michigan statutory will of

_____
(Full name)

According to section 2.2 of my Michigan statutory will and section 131a of the Revised Probate Code of Michigan, I give the following personal and household items to the persons designated below:

I sign my name to this separate list on_____, 19 _____ .

_____
(Signature)

SEPARATE LIST

for the Michigan statutory will of

_____
(Full name)

According to section 2.2 of my Michigan statutory will and section 131a of the Revised Probate Code of Michigan, I give the following personal and household items to the persons designated below:

I sign my name to this separate list on _____, 19 _____ .

_____
(Signature)